A Season in Turmoil

by Samuel Abt

VELOPRESS • BOULDER, COLORADO

Library of Congress Cataloging-in-Publication Data
Abt, Samuel.
    A Season in Turmoil / by Samuel Abt.
       p.   cm.
    ISBN 1-884737-09-9
    1. Armstrong, Lance 2. Cyclists-United States-Biography.
    3. LeMond, Greg 4. Bicycle racing. 5. Tour de France (Bicycle race) I. Title
    GV1051.A76A38 1996
    796.6'092--dc20
    [B]   96-11422
                                         CIP

PRINTED IN THE U.S.A.

VELOPRESS
1830 N. 55TH STREET
BOULDER COLORADO 80301-2700 USA
303/440-0601
303/444-6788 FAX
e-mail: velonews@aol.com

TO PURCHASE ADDITIONAL COPIES OF THIS BOOK
OR OTHER VELO PRODUCTS:
CALL 800/234-8356
INT'L 303/440-0601 EXT 6

COVER PHOTOS OF GREG LEMOND BY JOHN PIERCE
AND LANCE ARMSTRONG BY GRAHAM WATSON

This book is for Bob, Bertha and Kathy LeMond

Acknowledgments

For their help and friendship on the road and in the office, I owe thanks to many people. First is John Wilcockson, friend, traveling companion and editor. Others include Steve Wood, Rupert Guinness, Salvatore Zanca, Phil Liggett, Mike Price, Geoff Nicholson, Steve Bierley, Graham Jones, Tim Maloney and Marion Paull. As always, I owe special thanks to the editors in the sports department of *The New York Times*, and to my children, Claire, Phoebe and John, for their love.

CONTENTS

"If I watch them long enough
I see them come together,
I see them *placed*, I see them
engaged in this or that act and
in this or that difficulty.
How they look and move
and speak and behave,
always in the setting I have
found for them,
is my account
of them."

— *Ivan Turgenev,
as quoted by Henry James.*

Prologue: Dreaming about Tomorrow

MOST OF THE CROWD IN STROUDSBURG, PENNSYLVANIA, HAD GONE, and the beer party on a balcony near the finish line had moved indoors as the afternoon heat gave way to an early-evening chill. Banners were coming down and the grandstand was being dismantled with loud clangs as metal pipes dropped to the ground.

The winners and leaders had climbed the podium, received their jerseys and flowers, and climbed down again, dispersing. The bicycle race, a stage of the 1992 Tour DuPont through the Pocono Mountains, was over.

But not quite. It was over for only 86 of the 102 riders. Sixteen had been left far behind and were still out somewhere on the course, heading back to Stroudsburg and the finish line.

Although everything else was being packed away, there was still a finish line. A white strip covering electronic sensors, it would be the last thing to be stowed and moved to the next day's destination. As long as the finish line was still down across Main Street in Stroudsburg, the race continued.

The rules said no rider would be eliminated for a late finish, unless he came in more than 20 percent behind the time of the winner. In this case, since Uwe Preissler of the German national team won in five hours, one minute, 42 seconds, late finishers had a comfortable margin.

"I knew the field finished in five hours so I knew I had an hour to get across," said Jonas

Carney of the U.S. national team. "I just wanted to do that and look forward to another day. When you're that far back, all you keep thinking is that it's only one day and you've got to get through it.

"Sometimes it's the hardest thing you do, and the next day you turn it around." Carney finished 31 minutes, 58 seconds behind the winner.

One of the many charms of bicycle racing is how often, unlike what people are pleased to call real life, it offers that wonderful thing, a second chance.

Fail today in real life and the stain carries over to tomorrow and who knows how many more tomorrows. Fail today in bicycle racing and another chance to succeed arrives tomorrow. Or the day after tomorrow.

"I didn't feel very good to be that far behind, but you must go on, eh?" said Patrick Strouken, a Dutchman with the Collstrop team from Belgium. "Otherwise you're out of the race. When you're riding far behind, you keep thinking maybe tomorrow you'll have your chance." He finished 23:53 behind.

"I was having a hard day because my job was to do what I could for the team," explained David Farmer, a rider with Coors Light. To protect his team leader and the man in the yellow jersey, Dave Mann, Farmer helped set so fast a pace that he burned out two thirds of the way through the stage.

"I gave all I had, got dropped, and rode in to give another day," he said. "But it's hard. It's hard to have everybody see you back there. It's more than a little embarrassing, but that's what being a professional is all about." Farmer finished 23:02 behind.

"Embarrassed?" repeated Henri Manders, a Dutchman with the Helvetia team from Switzerland. "Why?" What then did Manders think about as he finished 11:01 behind? "About doing better the next day," he replied.

Main Street in Stroudsburg was nearly empty when suddenly a whistle sounded and the race announcer boomed the call of "rider up," as headlights appeared far down the street. It was the protective convoy.

Around the corner of Fifth Street, far past what may be the last Buster Brown shoe store in America, a group of riders struggled slowly toward the finish. Past the movie house that was offering an amateur production of "The Glass Menagerie" that night, past the original in the chain of Newberry variety stores, past the improbable gourmet store selling honey-flavored mustard to the Rust Belt came a small group of riders including Scott McKinley. Like Strouken, he finished 23:53 behind.

"I'm a sprinter and I get used to being dropped on climbs," McKinley explained the next morning as his Spago team began signing in for another stage. "When races are hilly, I'm just not competitive. So I have to be patient and wait for races that suit me.

"Just stick with it, don't get demoralized. I remind myself that I'll have plenty of races to win in the future."

On a stage into Hagerstown, Maryland, two days later, the terrain was mainly flat. McKinley began moving toward the front as the pack sped through the city. Into the last corner they came, and McKinley avoided a crash ahead to dig hard for the finish line.

This day was just short of the tomorrow that he was waiting for. Beaten by a couple of bicycle lengths, McKinley finished a fine second, which left him smiling.

"Told you," he said. "Wait a little while, your day has to come."

Then, as real life began to desert downtown Hagerstown and go home, workers started dismantling the grandstand, packing away the banners and stacking crowd barriers in trucks. One of the last few traces that a bicycle race had reached town was the finish line, still in place for any riders remaining out on the road … and dreaming about tomorrow.

[PART 1]

THE EARLY SEASON

1 Buds of Ambition

OUTSIDE, THE POPLAR TREES HAD LOST MOST OF THEIR LEAVES AND grapevines stood short and bare in dark fields. Inside, the talk was not of the approaching winter, but of spring. Ambition was sprouting inside.

Inside was the Diamond Suite of an undistinguished chain hotel just outside Bordeaux, one of the wine capitals of France. Despite its name, the Diamond Suite was a basic hotel conference room — white plaster walls, sturdy blue carpet, stackable chairs — where the GAN professional bicycle racing team was looking back, respectfully, at 1993 and ahead, hopefully, to 1994.

Team officials pronounced '93 a success: 23 victories, including the esteemed Paris-Roubaix classic and the lesser Paris-Brussels classic; the season-long Coupe de France; and two major time trials, the Grand Prix Eddy Merckx and the Chrono des Herbiers. GAN riders carried off bits and crumbs in other races: the climbing jersey and third place in the Dauphiné Libéré; second and third places in Paris-Nice; and victories in the prologues to the Route du Sud and the Tour de l'Ain.

Only the Tour de France was a disappointment. GAN riders did nothing in the world's richest, toughest and most prestigious bicycle road race and, as Greg LeMond said later, "Rightly or wrongly, riders are judged by how they do in the Tour de France." Teams too.

Nobody was actually blaming LeMond for the disappointment, but the team's

Tour hopes rested entirely on him. His teammates rode to support him and there was not a potential winner among them. So, when a mysterious pollen allergy left him too exhausted to enter the race, the deflated GAN team rode as if it knew it had no chance.

That was 1993, which was dwindling into darkness and frost outside the hotel near Bordeaux. Inside, looking fit and rested, acting friendly and buoyant, talking optimistically about 1994, LeMond sat in the front row at the GAN team presentation. He had flown from the United States to France the day before and would return home in two days. He looked natty in a tweed jacket, black turtleneck sweater and pale blue jeans, entirely different from the team uniform of gray jacket, gray shirt, gray pants and off-gray floral tie. LeMond kept trying not to yawn, despite his jet lag. In his enthusiasm, he seemed far younger than the 33 he would turn at his next birthday in June.

Despite his bleak record for the last three years, he remained an undisputed star: After the official presentation of GAN's 18 riders for the next season, most of them congregated at the bar, eating hors d'oeuvres, sipping champagne and chatting with each other, while most of the reporters and photographers met with LeMond. His French is fluent, his explanations articulate if sometimes contradictory and his manner polished. There are a few dark sides to his story but, no longer the young man yearning for understanding, he knows how to keep them hidden.

Looking bemused, Roger Legeay, the team's directeur sportif, regarded the mass interview from the other end of the room. A former rider of no particular distinction himself, Legeay is proud of his eye for talent. When he offered LeMond a job during the 1989 Tour, the rider was still recovering from the hunting accident that left him near death in a field in northern California more than two years earlier and seemed unable to regain the form he displayed in winning the 1986 Tour de France. Down and written off by all except Legeay, LeMond won his first race in years the next day and went on to win that Tour on its final day. The next year, riding this time for Legeay, he won again.

They had disagreed occasionally about training and about salary, but Legeay's affection for LeMond was as obvious as the hearty clasp around the waist with which he greeted the rider he had not seen since June, when a suffering LeMond withdrew from the Giro d'Italia and went home to Minnesota to mend. Then, in July, he fell during a training ride as he crossed a railroad track and broke the scaphoid bone in his right wrist, ending his season.

"I've had some up and down periods, true," LeMond said as he discussed his morale. "Through July and August, I have to say I was down." With relish, he then described his ideal summer, far from his occupation as a professional bicycle racer paid about $1 million a year: "I went to Montana two times fishing, stayed home, we decorated our house. I just did stuff I'd been wanting to do and never had the time to do. I tell you it felt good to have two months where I didn't have to think about training. It went by too fast."

In August, he went fishing with his older son, Geoffrey, who was then nine. "Geoffrey and I, a great trip, just me with my son. It was the best trip I've ever taken." Geoffrey caught 25 fish in a week, mainly trout and whitefish, LeMond continued excitedly. He caught 30 himself one day. "Fly-fishing, you catch a lot if you hit the right fly — you match the hatch."

"It was the worst year for my cycling, but the best year for my family. Even in March, I was going so bad that I had to stay home and train. April we were together," because so many of that month's classics, or one-day races, are near the LeMonds' house in Belgium, "May and June except for the Tour of Italy, August, September, October — it was great." He has often been charged with being more interested in family life than in training.

Legeay was outlining LeMond's program for 1994: the Ruta Mexico, Paris-Nice, the Tour of Flanders, Paris-Roubaix, Liège-Bastogne-Liège, the Tour DuPont, the Dauphiné Libéré and the Tour of Switzerland, all of them leading once more to the Tour de France.

Did he think LeMond still had a chance to win the Tour?

"I think it will be very difficult for him," he responded. "But it will be possible for him to influence the Tour.

"What we really want for Greg is for him to leave cycling next year — if he decides to leave cycling — like the great champion he is, with some good victories next season. We want him to leave by *la grande porte*," the front door, not just slip out the back and be gone without notice.

"He seems very motivated," Legeay added.

A listener could not help saying, "It's only November."

Legeay broke into a laugh. "Fair enough," he admitted. "Fair enough."

Nowhere near fair, LeMond retorted later. Motivation was not the problem, he insisted, preparation was. "I know about training," he said, "I wrote a book about training. But I got away from what I used to do. I was doing cross-country skiing and easy riding in the winter and I'm starting to go in the opposite way now, working on my power, lifting weights with my legs, working on increasing my oxygen consumption. I'm watching my weight.

"I need to build my power and strength up as high as I can and then worry about my endurance. Endurance is the easiest aspect to build up. What I'm doing now is the opposite of what I've been doing, always working on my endurance. Except in 1989, when I did a lot of power training in the winter, and that year I had great results as early as February.

"I'm not going to rush," he continued. "I'm going to build up slowly, that's my goal, to really have a good base so that when I start racing hard in February, March and April, my body doesn't get tired from it and I get better. Which hasn't been the case the last couple of years."

By now, LeMond was sitting at a table in the infield at the Bordeaux velodrome, watching the six-day race and eating dinner. He was also signing autographs, posing for photographs, and firing the starting pistol for one of the events. He had come such a long way since he was always introduced as "the American," the great novelty in the European sport of bicycle racing a decade before. Now he was a three-time winner of the Tour de France and a two-time world champion in the professional road race. LeMond needed no introduction now other than his name.

Training was still on his mind as he returned to the table after posing for yet more photographs. This time he was flanked by two other Tour winners, Bernard Thévenet, who won in 1975 and 1977, and Lucien Aimar, who won in 1966. Other than Miguel Indurain, the Spaniard who had won the last three Tours de France, there was no man still riding who had won as many Tours as LeMond.

"I might have the same enthusiasm for racing that I had all those years ago," he said, reflecting on his years as a professional, "but not the same enthusiasm for training. And just a 10-percent difference in training could make a total difference in the way you race. I'm trying to change that this winter."

After he returned to the United States in a few days, he planned to leave his home in Minnesota and move to San Diego, to begin training in warm weather. "I'll be out there a month and a half," he said, "November 20 to December 20, come home for 10 days for the holidays, then go back out January 1, stay out two more weeks, then do the Tour of Mexico." He was scheduled to return to Europe for the new season in mid-February.

His wife and three children would be joining him in California for only a week, he noted pointedly.

"You've got to be in good shape for next year," he said, speaking of himself. "You've got to be well prepared. I want to have as successful a season as I can next year and I'll do my best but....

"It's going to be a very, very hard Tour de France. It's going to be a year of unknowns. It's going to be an eye-opener. I'm not certain how I can perform. I haven't performed in two years almost."

He paused to sign an autograph, then spent a few moments watching races on the track. For somebody who, as he says, wrote a book about training, he seemed uncertain about his own methods.

"I got away from what I used to do," he repeated. "In 1992, I had a good season until the Tour de France, but I overraced, overtrained. Then in '93, because my winter preparation was poor, I was training to try to catch up with everybody and I got myself in pretty good shape by April, but maybe went into the Tour of Italy a little overtrained, a little tired. And then with the pollen, I got a big cold virus on my mouth and lips midway through, and it was enough to get my body totally wiped out.

"For six weeks after the Tour of Italy, I had low cortisone levels, low testosterone levels, extreme fatigue, symptoms of Chronic Fatigue Syndrome.

"Is bread on your left or your right?" he suddenly asked, taking a roll from the plate on his right and beginning to eat it. It was past 9:30 p.m. and dinner had not yet been served.

"I almost stopped breathing one day in the Tour of Italy," he resumed. "I think there's something in Italy I'm not treated for — all the trees, something down there. Also I'm really allergic to grasses, and it was a warm period and people were cutting grass. I'm getting treated for that now, so I should be a little better next year." His father-in-law, he noted, is an immunologist, which is handy for a man with as many allergies as LeMond has.

"Anyway, it took four weeks to start to feel better and then when I began training again, I broke my hand and decided to take my break for two months until I had my cast off."

He had not paid much attention to the Tour de France that July, he admitted, following results now and again in the Minneapolis newspaper. Nor had he given much thought to the world championship road race, which he won in 1983 and 1989. "I wasn't in shape even to wish I'd been there," LeMond said. "I don't want to go to races where I'm not ready."

He praised Lance Armstrong, the American rider who won the world professional road race championship. "What he did, I think, was fabulous. He's only

21 years old and to win the world's his first year as a pro is remarkable. Lance has already proven himself as a great rider and he should have many more good years. I'm near retirement and somebody's got to be there to keep pro cycling alive in America.

"Can he win the Tour? You can't even say yet what his capabilities are, what his capabilities will be in five years. He might be able to blow away everybody. Or he might just be a great one-day racer."

Dinner had arrived, with the first course a mushroom mousse topped with a slice of fish. LeMond dug in, sipping slowly from his glass of white wine.

Would the coming year be his last? So many big names among his contemporaries — Laurent Fignon, Stephen Roche and Sean Kelly — had either announced their retirement or were considering doing so. "I don't know," he replied. "I'm giving it serious thought. The ideal situation, if America had more races, would be to race there in '95 and then until the Olympics. I'd love to do it. I might not dominate, but I'd love to go to the Olympics. But if I have a good year next year, I'd also like to stop, finish on a high note.

"Does it matter if I finish on a high note? What do you think," he asked, startlingly. "What do you think I should do?"

LeMond seemed to expect an answer but, getting none, continued talking. "Your body can be perfect, but a lot goes on in your head," he said. "These last two years, I have not been at my best. When you're not, it's hard to climb. If I could just get my weight down to 69 or 68 kilos (150 pounds).

"It's not just weight," he decided, "but weight and training. It's proper training.

"Everybody says the last two years are because of my age. I am convinced it's not my age. What would have changed in my body in three years? Nothing! The problem is that as you get older you have a lot more distractions, a lot more demands on your time. It's not age. All it takes is having the right combination: no stress, good training."

As the riders spun by on the track and the crowd began screaming encouragement, LeMond became transformed. No longer that classic case of an athlete unable to believe that his body cannot perform the prodigies of a decade before and cannot accept the pain and sacrifice that bicycle racing demands, he was suddenly the 20-year-old beginner, his teeth still in braces, his hair still blond, his dreams of someday winning the Tour de France still private. He was not the fading veteran now but once again the hottest thing on wheels and eager to prove it.

"It's not age," he declared firmly. "In '92, I cross-country skied so much in the winter and raced so much in the mid-season up to the Tour that I died there because I was burned out. Last year, opposite. I had such distractions during the winter that I couldn't hardly train and I tried rushing myself back into shape, got sick and it blew me out. It's not age. It's been a lot of things I've done that haven't prepared me for the season."

He was willing to do it differently now? He was prepared to make the same sacrifices he made those long years ago when he was winning the Tour de France?

"I'm going to California in five days, right?" he answered. Right.

✺

One man not making sacrifices anymore was LeMond's former Tour de France rival, Laurent Fignon. Although the same age as LeMond, the Frenchman had already quit cycling....

THAT METEOR, THAT LIGHTNING BOLT LAURENT FIGNON HAD BLAZED out. Riding in a minor French race late in the summer of 1993, Fignon coasted to the side of the road halfway through and got off his bicycle for the last time as a professional. The authority for that was Fignon himself, and he could be believed.

Blazed out or burned out, how to decide? What could be said was that after a dozen years of majestic heights — two victories in the Tour de France, one in the Giro d'Italia, two in Milan-San Remo, a French national championship; and profound depths — a heel injury that cost him peak seasons, last-stage losses of both the Tour and the Giro, two positive drug findings — at age 33, Fignon had retired as a racer. He had no further ambition, unlike Greg LeMond, who rode with him on the Renault team in the early 1980s before the American decided that two young leaders were one too many and, after finishing third to Fignon in the 1984 Tour, left for La Vie Claire.

The Frenchman went out his own way, announcing beforehand that since he had no interest in competing in the world championships, the Grand Prix Ouest-France would be his farewell. He would have retired quietly, he said, but he owed it to the fans to be there.

The statement was pure Fignon: An arrogance that was almost touching in its naïveté. Or, if you wish, a naïveté that was almost dumbfounding in its arrogance. By the time he retired, nobody came to see just him. The rider ranked 201st in the world considered himself a fan attraction? The rider whose sole victory that year came in the Ruta de Mexico in February? A two-page photograph in *Vélo* magazine, the bible of bicycle racing in France, inadvertently said it all. There in the foreground was Fignon, the familiar ponytail, the familiar granny glasses, the familiar strained look, and there in the background were five fans — all looking down the road away from Fignon.

Besides the photograph and a brief text block, *Vélo* had little else to say about his retirement. Not so long ago, a rider who recorded 76 victories in his career, including nine stage victories in the Tour de France, would have been given a proper sendoff of a long article, perhaps even a cover photograph and half a page of tributes. Now *Vélo* and French fans have mountain biking on their mind, with the magazine giving the off-road discipline 20 of its 70 pages in the issue with Fignon's retirement.

Time had moved quickly since 1982, when Fignon emerged from an obscure amateur career and startlingly won the Critérium International in one of his first races as a professional with the juggernaut Renault team. Bernard Hinault was the Renault leader then (LeMond was simply a young hope) and the French were still crazy about road racing. In the years since, the last Frenchman to win the Tour was Hinault, in 1985. The year Fignon quit, no Frenchman finished higher than 15th and only one Frenchman, a rider for an Andorran team, won a stage.

Other sports besides mountain biking had captured the young: The same newsstand that sold *Vélo* and two other road-racing magazines offered four French magazines about mountain-biking, five about professional basketball in America, four about golf, and even two about wrestling. None of these could have been found when Fignon was sweeping the Tour de France and the country was glorying in his triumph.

He was not speaking publicly after his retirement and so, to know his thoughts, a fan had to look back to the interview he gave to *L'Équipe*, the daily French sports newspaper, the day he quit. From the beginning of the interview, he was vintage Fignon, remote and brusque. Not for lack of trying was he voted the *citron* (lemon) prize for rudeness when he won the Giro d'Italia in 1989.

Had it meant something to him to start his last race? the reporter from *L'Équipe* asked.

"Something?" Fignon repeated. "No, why should I have felt something?"

Not a heavy heart or sweaty palms?

"No. There was no reason for me to feel sad. I'm rather happy to retire. I decided on this many months ago and I started thinking about it two years ago. Since

I signed with Gatorade (before the 1992 season), I knew I was joining my last team. Only the dead are sad and, as far as I'm concerned, don't talk about a burial but about the start of a new life. So don't be sad for me. What would have been sad was for me to continue, to keep quitting at the first feed zone, to finish a little like Eddy Merckx, who so badly ended his career...."

You say you're fed up. With what?

"With everything. Fed up with cycling, with a world where all you see is the same people ... with everything."

And what are your plans?

"I'm going to stay far away from the world of cycling next year, but I'll probably be back afterward, although I don't know in what capacity."

Do you fear that you'll be remembered more for your failures than your successes?

"Fear, no, I'm not afraid. People will remember whatever they want to, it won't mean anything to me."

Cold, defensive and ungrateful: Let us now praise famous men. Fignon won the Tour de France twice, in 1983 as a virtual unknown, and in 1984 when everybody went gunning for him. A month after he lost the Giro in the final day's time trial, when Francesco Moser introduced his aerodynamic bicycle to overtake him, Fignon overpowered the field in the '84 Tour de France, winning five stages. The victory was a demonstration of sheer dominance such as the pack witnesses only from a Merckx, an Hinault, an Indurain — and only in their prime.

And then, just 24 years old, he was struck down. An operation for tendinitis in his left heel sidelined him for most of 1985 and not for years afterward did he truly recover. In 1988, he won Milan-San Remo and the next year he was back on top: first again in the Italian classic, first in the Giro and first in the Tour ... until the final day, when LeMond beat him by 58 seconds in the time trial and by eight seconds overall.

Everybody remembers the photographs of a spent Fignon slumped and weeping on the Champs-Elysées after he crossed the finish to find himself a runner-up. Few remember that he placed third in the fastest time trial in the long history of the Tour de France. What people forget now is that he went down fighting.

Fignon was always good at fighting — but often it was verbally and with rivals, the press and the fans. He mocked Hinault and LeMond, he struck photographers and refused to speak with reporters. At the end of his career, it seemed clear that Fignon really was always fighting with himself.

He raged. Fignon was not so much a French rider as a Paris rider, and there is a clear distinction to be made here. French riders are Charly Mottets, Thierry Claveyrolats, Pascal Linos, Gilles Delions, Laurent Jalaberts, Frédéric Moncassins, Eric Boyers, Eric Caritouxs and Bruno Cornillets ... even Marc Madiots and Gilbert Duclos-Lassalles. They are generally well-mannered and soft-spoken, uncomplaining and accommodating. They win races, but they are never winners in Fignon's class. They are formed young, burdened by the heavy satchel that all French schoolchildren wear on their shoulders to pack books even to first grade. See, French society appears to be saying, we all have a weight to carry through life.

Once in a while, though, a French rider throws off the weight and expresses that most admired and most feared attitude: character. Hinault was famous for his character. "I race to win, not to please people," he often said.

Like Hinault, Fignon had an excess of character. Born just outside Paris and a longtime resident of the capital, he was the archetypal Parisian, indifferent to everybody but himself. When foreigners say the French are rude or self-centered or self-serving, they rarely mean the French; they mean Parisians. Outside Paris, foreigners are startled to find the French can be kind and even unselfish.

Fignon took victories from teammates (the Tour of the European Community), chased them down (the 1989 world championship), treated them like hired hands and made few friends in the pack. He was respected, and at his peak feared, but not admired. He was Parisian to his fingertips and not many would miss him. He was also a champion, and the sport, especially in France, needs more riders like him.

2 The Man in the Rainbow Jersey

ONE PHOTOGRAPHER WAS UP A LADDER WITH A CAMERA, ANOTHER was walking around with a light meter, calling out numbers as he scanned members of the Motorola bicycle team. They were posed in front of a disused roadside chapel in Tuscany. In 1993, the team photograph was taken in a warehouse for a high-tech look and so, yin and yang, in 1994 the goal was something picturesque, even touristic. "But elegant," one of the photographers explained.

Center front among the 18 riders, the four team officials, four or five bicycles and a team car stood Lance Armstrong.

He deserved the position of honor: Armstrong was the team leader and he wore the rainbow-striped jersey of the world professional road-race champion. In his first full season as a professional the year before, he won the world championship, a stage of the Tour de France, the U.S. professional championship, and a $1 million prize by finishing first in all three events of an American race series.

Winners stand center front.

Then why, in the warehouse photograph taken early in 1993, when Armstrong had appeared as a professional in just half-a-dozen races, was he also center front?

"I was the team leader a little bit last year," the 22-year-old Texan said in February 1994, in the Italian village of Castagneto Carducci, where his team was holding a training camp. "I was certainly the team leader at the Tour DuPont and throughout the million-dollar saga. In the Tour de France, I had days where I was considered the man."

That didn't wash. All those races took place months after the photograph. Who knew so early that Armstrong had such star quality? He smiled broadly and ducked his head in mock humility. If anybody knew, Armstrong knew.

"I was always worried about not failing. I wanted to win, but more than that, I didn't want to fail. And," he spoke slowly now, "I don't think I have."

He was determined, he continued, not to fail while he was world champion, a title that is decided every summer in a one-day race.

"Over the last few years, people seem to think the rainbow jersey has had a curse upon it," he noted. The 1990 world champion, Rudy Dhaenens of Belgium, never won another race and had retired from the sport. The 1991 and 1992 champion, Gianni Bugno of Italy, failed to win another major race during those two years.

Armstrong hoped to end that spell soon, as early as the first classic of the spring, the long race from Milan to San Remo in Italy. "It's a big goal for me, because it's the first big race that anybody's paying attention to, and I've heard so much talk about world champions wearing the rainbow jersey and not being able to perform in the jersey. This is going to be an event where I can showcase not only my talent but the possibilities of the rainbow jersey winning a big one.

"As a champion, you have to represent yourself well and your team and your sponsor well, but with the rainbow jersey you're also representing the sport and the jersey itself. With that comes added pressure tenfold."

How much of that added pressure tenfold was he feeling?

"None," he said flatly.

When he first began making a name for himself as a member of the U.S. national amateur team four years previously, Armstrong was regarded as arrogant. Then he started fulfilling his promise by winning races, and what seemed arrogant became brash. As a professional, what seemed brash became confident, ebullient, even charming and honest.

"There's no pressure because I'm prepared," he explained. "I'm ready. I've said that all along in my career — I've always said I'm ready, I'm ready, I can do this and I'm confident.

"Now I truly feel I'm secure with myself and my career. I realize I can have success. I know it's right there. It's not anything I'm worried about. It's just a matter of going out and doing it. I still have the desire to do it, like I've always had, but now

I know in my heart and my mind that I can conquer this sport and that I can conquer the races."

He had felt pressure, though. "Not from the team and not from the sport, not from my friends and not from my family. But I felt a little pressure from myself because it seems I demand a little more from myself than others do."

The second youngest man ever to be world pro champion, Armstrong also appeared to be a little more worried about his reception in the rainbow jersey than he should have been. He confessed that he scented a certain resentment among riders on other teams.

"Maybe 'resentment' is too strong, maybe I'm looking at it in a pessimistic way and I shouldn't," he said. "I'm sure there are people who are jealous."

Yet, with the season just beginning, he had not been in contact with many other riders. That did not dissuade him.

Armstrong was reminded that no less a racer than Miguel Indurain, the reigning Tour de France champion and the second-place rider in the world championship, said afterward that Armstrong deserved the victory because he was obviously the strongest man that day.

"Not everybody has the class of Indurain," he replied.

"Surely they're a little bit jealous," he said again of other riders. "I think most of them are thinking maybe it was a fluke, thinking it was a little bit lucky."

He did not agree. "I don't think it was lucky. I rode a great race."

He remembered when he knew he had won: "When I turned around, four or five kilometers to go, and just saw nobody.... I turned around and didn't see anybody, and the last split I heard was about 20 seconds.

"I couldn't believe it. I thought, 'Oh my God, I'm going to win the world championship.' Then I thought, 'Oh no, I've got another lap because this is too good to be true.' I said to myself, 'How am I going to know? I don't want to cross the line and keep going.'

"It was all starting to happen so fast. From that point on, it just all happened so quick. I said, 'I'll check the computer' and I did and it said 250 and I said, 'Oh my God, this is it.' And I thought, 'Hopefully, the computer isn't wrong.'"

It wasn't. He won the 257-kilometer race in Oslo by 19 seconds, a big lead, and finished by blowing kisses to the crowd.

"To everybody, everybody there, the fans, the spectators," he said. "And they liked it. Before I was blowing kisses, they were sitting down and afterward they were standing up. You have to please the fans.

"That's part of my ideas about cycling: It's a sport, it's entertainment, sports are entertainment. You can win and not be entertaining, but I think people leave a race with a better image of the sport if it's entertaining.

"I'm here not just to do things for myself and Motorola but to promote the sport. I want people to leave and say, 'Hey, I can't wait to go to another bike race.'"

After the race, officials tried to take the new champion to meet the King of Norway but Armstrong refused to go along unless his mother, Linda Waller, who watches some of his races in Europe, could come, too. "She was thrilled, she was thrilled for me." At each of many checkpoints, he had to argue security men into allowing his mother to pass through. "They kept saying only the winner can come, but I told them, 'If she's not coming, I'm not coming.'" Finally, they were in a room where she watched her son shake hands with a king.

That was a long way from Plano, Texas, where Armstrong grew up as the fatherless child of a 17-year-old girl. "Were we poor?" he asked, repeating a question. "No, but I certainly didn't have a silver spoon." He was warned that another personal question was coming: Had it been a long time since he had contact with his father? "Forever," he answered. "It's a personal question but I don't take it personally."

"She's been remarried not that long ago, but she's been with her husband quite a long time and she loves him and I know he loves her and I care a lot for him and that's all that matters. She's happy and I'm happy. As far as I'm concerned, biology doesn't matter."

Usually a man of many words, Armstrong used just one when asked if his mother had been supportive. "Very," he said.

"It means more to me than just having her at a race," he continued. "It gives me the opportunity to spend time with her before the race or after the race, allowing her the opportunity to spectate the race. It's not a normal relationship anyway, being that she's young and she had me very young and she grew up at the same time I was growing up and we sort of grew up as friends and not as mother and son.

"So I grew up as one of her friends and when I'm not there all the time she really feels...." He thought about it. "Lonely," he decided.

Loneliness, any sort of unhappiness, troubles Armstrong. "I'm looking for cycling to make my life, I'm not looking for cycling to ruin my life. For some people, it's certainly ruined their life or made it miserable. I've seen some cyclists that just don't appear very happy. That's the last thing I want.

"I want to be happy, I want cycling to make me happy, I want it to make my family happy and right now it's doing that. The day it doesn't is the day I'm going to stop. I'm very happy now, though."

A contributing factor to his happiness is the big money he began earning once he won the world championship; his salary reportedly rose tenfold to $750,000 a year.

"Everybody likes money," he said strongly. "There's nothing wrong with money. There's nothing wrong with using money as a motivation. It should be a motivation not only for athletes but for everyday people. In America, people look badly on money and don't consider it an incentive, which it is. I'm supermotivated by money.

"I'm not going to sit here and say money doesn't mean anything to me, because it means a lot. And I enjoy giving it back. As much as I enjoy getting money, I love to give money. Christmastime, obviously a time you give and get, I don't really care to get anything, I've got everything I've ever wanted, but I like to give away stuff."

Armstrong lives now in Austin, Texas, where he hopes to stay permanently, liking both the training its nearby hills offer and the relaxation of its many music clubs. A fan of Stevie Ray Vaughan and Travis Tritt, Armstrong plays the acoustic guitar, but admits that he does not practice it.

He remains virtually unknown in Austin despite his world championship. "If I go into a club in Austin, people don't come over for autographs," he said. "They don't know who I am." He seemed unbothered, although he added that he half expected to be called to the White House to be congratulated by President Clinton. "Guess he was busy," Armstrong said. Nearly the only reaction back home to his victory, he continued, was the time a policeman pulled him over while he was riding his bicycle and asked for an autograph.

Endorsements did not flow in either. "Out of the sport, no," Armstrong said. "That was okay. Right now, I'm more concerned with my career, focusing on my career, not only in the season but, more importantly, in the wintertime. If you're going to do endorsements, if you're going to travel around and do appearances, you're going to do that in the winter. And I was not interested in doing that this winter because I was too concerned with defending this jersey, wearing this jersey like it should be worn." Starting early in November, he said, he had ridden nearly 7000 kilometers in training — double the usual amount — although he admitted that the training had been inconsistent: "a lot of heavy weeks and then hardly anything at all."

He was optimistic about his form and opportunities in the coming season. "I'm learning more and gaining more as far as tactics are concerned," he judged. "In the past, I've been very aggressive and sometimes overly aggressive and I regret it. Certainly. But sometimes you make some mistakes when you're aggressive. I recognize those mistakes and won't make them again.

"So my style may appear to change but it will have the same aggression with a little more intelligence."

After more than a month of tune-up races, mainly in Italy, he was to get his chance to convince doubters — real or imagined — in the first of the season's World Cup classics, Milan-San Remo. It is a special race to him because its distance, 297 kilometers, suits a rider with his strength, aggression and stamina and because he was near the front in 1993 until the final climb of the Poggio, where he faded.

Armstrong explained that he had not ridden his own race then but had been working for a teammate, Max Sciandri of Italy, who had since joined the GB-MG team. "I was left a chance to take any opportunity, if something happened to him or he was having a bad day. At the finish, I was definitely working for him because he was there and he was feeling good and he wanted help." Sciandri finished third, Armstrong 22nd.

Now the team would work for Armstrong.

"I have a great relationship with this team," he said. "I count them as my friends, my best friends. And they look at me the same way. The neat thing is that the way they act toward me and the way I act toward them hasn't changed a bit. I'm still the same person with a different jersey."

As a leader, he continued, his big job is to motivate. "Head up troops," he said. "I like to think I'm a motivator. I get supermotivated myself and I feel that I can motivate.

"We're all on the same level here, so it's very easy for them to relate to me, to see when I'm hurting. They see when I want something, when I want to win it, even if I don't tell them.

"Sometimes I tell them, sometimes I say some things in the races and I think it gets them psyched up — how great I'm feeling or how I'm going to win. Within a race, I can boldly predict to my teammates, 'Hey, I'm going to win today, guys.' Before a stage or during. I think they like that.

"Certainly that's a little bit confident, but I think if you're saying it within the team it's a little different than if you're blurting it in headlines. But it motivates the guys.

"Another thing that motivates them is that when they have worked for me, have sacrificed for me, the majority of the time I've come through. So when it comes around the next time and I say, 'Come on guys, we've got to chase, do some work here, I need some help,' these guys are 100-percent willing to do it, because they know if anybody is going to come through for them, it's going to be me.

"And the day I can't do that is the day I need to stop racing. I don't want to let anybody down. And that's part of my motivation, that when I say, 'Okay guys, let's work,' they get up there and they're on the front hammering, chasing down somebody, leading me out.

"I see these guys hurting, I see the salt forming on their shorts, I see them sweating, I hear them breathing and that motivates me.

"I'm willing to sacrifice for them. I've shown in the past that I'm willing to work for somebody else if I'm not riding well. That's not a problem. I've displayed that and I'll continue to do that. Nobody thinks that a rainbow jersey can ride on the front for his teammates, but I don't have a problem with that. If I was in a position where I had to work for somebody else, sure."

❋

FOR DR. MASSIMO TESTA, THE MOTOROLA TEAM TRAINING CAMP was an opportunity to tune up what he called his riders' aerobic engines. For Andy Hampsten, it was a start on polishing his climbing talent. For John Hendershot, it was a time to reaccustom riders to massage. For Lance Armstrong, it was a chance "to see the guys who made you what you are" and to focus on defending his rainbow jersey. For Jim Ochowicz, it was two weeks to review his riders' personal and team goals. For Phil Anderson, it was the safety of riding far from hostile traffic. For Paul Sherwen, it was an opportunity to have publicity photos taken and to accommodate requests for interviews. For Stephen Swart, it was a chance to meet his new teammates and "start to fit in." For Carlo Guarguaglini, it was the memory of his days as a racer in the Giro d'Italia, Vuelta a España and Tour de France, 30 years ago. For Scott Parr, it was a time to adjust new bicycles to any changes in position that riders decided to make during the winter. And for Sean Yates, it was riding in a crowd. "You get a feeling for riding with other guys," Yates said. "It's not like a sudden jump from riding on your own during the winter to screaming around the peloton with 200 people."

The two-week training camp that the Motorola team organized in Tuscany just as the new season began was indeed many things to many people. To all of them, though, it seemed to be an unqualified success.

"We've been very pleased with the training, it's been very consistent," said

Ochowicz, Motorola's general manager. "Super," said Hampsten. "We're completely relaxed, we're having a blast."

"It was time for a change," Ochowicz noted as he explained why the team had shifted its training camp, after six years in Santa Rosa, California. "It was good for us when we were there, but we needed a change. This gives us a chance to start the camp a little earlier and get the guys over jet lag and the other things that put us at a little bit of a disadvantage. When the camp is over, we're ready to start racing."

Sherwen, Motorola's publicity director, amplified this: "It's a lot more logical to train in Europe, since when we trained on the West Coast, we headed to Europe almost for the first race. Guys from America needed more time to get settled for the season in Europe. And we had a little bit of bad luck with the weather in Santa Rosa — we were caught in the floods last year."

The team's luck was better in Tuscany where the weather was nearly perfect: clear and brisk (the mid-50s during the day) for more than a week, colder and occasionally rainy thereafter. Another major advantage was the sparse traffic on the roads around the team's base in Castagneto Carducci, about 35 miles south of Livorno and a couple of miles inland from the Ligurian Sea.

"The terrain is the same as Santa Rosa, but the big plus is the lack of traffic, hostile traffic," felt Phil Anderson, the Australian rider. "In California, people seemed envious of seeing cyclists out — maybe they got beaten by their wives before they left their homes — and they sort of took it out on anybody they saw out there ... forcing us off the road, honking us. Even the police would be telling us to get single file, abusing us for holding up traffic. Here, when we go by, the police clap at us."

The distractions were fewer, too. The Ti' Martino, a new, two-story hotel that was the team's base, had a lot going for it; but nobody could ever accuse the hotel of being bright lights-big city, since watching the Leghorn chickens scratching in the dirt next door can be a major diversion for guests. Balancing that, the hotel's restaurant has an excellent kitchen that specializes in cooking meat over a wood fire in the Tuscan manner.

"The food here is exceptional," gushed Sherwen, as he sat down to a dinner of homemade pasta, grilled chicken with deep-fried artichokes, and then a gooey dessert. "Dr. Testa is in the kitchen all the time, telling them how he wants the food cooked. It's a little family hotel, owned by a guy (Guarguaglini) who was a pro rider (from 1959 to 1962 with the EMI team in Italy) ... and they can't do enough for us."

"It's much calmer here than in Santa Rosa, no distractions," agreed Yates, the British rider. "We just ride the bikes, rest in the afternoon, have a massage, eat and sleep. In Santa Rosa, we ate out at night, walked around town, went to the cinema — not really 100-percent serious as we are here."

Norman Alvis used nearly the same words. "We get a lot of time to train because there are no distractions here," the American rider agreed. "I don't run into town to buy something because I'm in America, or go to the movies. Basically I get up, eat, ride, come back, have a nap, have a massage, eat again and concentrate on my training."

Training camp is also quality time for the support staff. Hendershot, the chief soigneur, explained the special importance of massage at the beginning of the season: "Normally during the winter, most riders don't receive regular massage. During training camp, because their bodies are slowly becoming accustomed to longer and longer rides, the massage is very important to recovery. But because they haven't had massage all winter, their legs can be very tender, and so they need to begin getting used to body work again.

"It's like if you have ticklish feet and you tickle them a little bit every day, eventually that sensitivity goes away." Riders were massaged every other day for 45 minutes to an hour — about a third longer than a session during a race — by one of the three soigneurs in camp. "Without massage, you don't recover as fast," Hendershot explained. "And that's the name of the game in cycling: recovery. Whoever recovers fastest does the best."

For the mechanics, said Parr, the camp allows a chance not only to get to know riders better but also to make all the small adjustments they want on their new bicycles. "Fifty to 75 percent of the riders change their (frame) geometry slightly, and you need to change everything to maintain the same position," he said. Armstrong, for example, decided to move his saddle forward about a centimeter on his road bike and a bit more than that on his time-trial machine.

The hotel, which features over its reception desk a huge photograph of its owner straining in a race, is accustomed to all this activity. The Lampre team, led by Maurizio Fondriest, stayed there in 1993 and returned to the area to train for the new season. Two other Italian teams also trained nearby, with GB-MG, headed by Johan Museeuw, just minutes away and Mercatone Uno, headed by Mario Cipollini, farther afield.

Certainly the setting was ideal, a cyclo-tourist's dream: avenues of cypress trees and umbrella pines lining the flat roads near the coast and the hills behind the motel; flowering almond trees in many yards; farmhouses painted a light lime or pale yellow; fields of vines for the region's wines; and workmen pruning olive trees — the idea seems to be to open them to the sun, to let light reach the inner branches — and burning the debris at the side of the road.

But nobody was at the training camp for the scenery. As Dr. Testa said, "The main goal of a training camp is to make the body ready for the physical situation of a race. The camp is all about the capability to perform. It's not too difficult to reach a good level of condition, but it's difficult to keep that good level."

So, he continued, his programs for the riders emphasize long endurance, fast endurance, training the aerobic engine — increasing the input of oxygen to the muscles by increasing heartbeats — and building the anaerobic threshold, that level where lactic acid forms an insufferable wall. "In a race, you have to follow wheels — you cannot slow down when you hit your threshold," he said.

As preparation for the camp, he had already prescribed training programs for the off-season between the middle of October and the beginning of February. Riders were advised to show up with between 3000 and 3500 kilometers in their legs, although Armstrong said he had logged 7000.

Dr. Testa had two basic programs for the training camp, one for the riders who would soon be engaged in the spring classics and one for longer-term results: "Riders who do classics work harder now than the climbers in the big Tours." Motorola would race the Giro d'Italia in May and June and the Tour de France in July. While those two tours were among the team's major goals, they shared priorities with the World Cup classics, the Tour DuPont and the world championships, Ochowicz explained.

He made it plain that the point of the training camp was work, to prepare for the 200 days of racing ahead. Riders were asked not to bring their wives or girlfriends, although they were allowed at an optional, follow-up camp on the French Riviera later in the month.

Ochowicz had high hopes for the Motorola team, which he helped form in 1981 as an amateur team under the sponsorship of 7-Eleven and which turned professional in 1985. Motorola took over the sponsorship in 1992 and was signed through 1994, with an option on 1995.

The team's 18 riders represented 12 nationalities, most of them from Motorola's markets. That diversity, plus new riders, demanded early coordination. "We have a lot of meetings here," Ochowicz said. "That gives us a chance to review goals and brief riders on all kinds of things — getting to races, what clothes to wear, what we expect of them. The new ones don't know, the old ones forget."

A typical schedule was posted on a door of the equipment truck: "Tuesday, 110 Ks, 3-4 hours; Wednesday, 130 Ks; Thursday, 70 Ks morning, 2 hours intervals, 2 minutes 90 percent, 2 minutes slow; Friday, 90 Ks; Saturday, 170 Ks, easy up and down; Sunday, tests, training in small groups."

This was Saturday and 17 of the 18 racers — all except Frankie Andreu, who had the flu — were gathering in front of the hotel and preparing to set off. Hennie Kuiper, their directeur sportif, was starting with them and Ochowicz, a member of the 1972 and 1976 U.S. Olympic pursuit team, had left a good five — or was that 10? — minutes before. When the road almost immediately began winding uphill, it was obvious why Ochowicz needed the head start. But why did he need the ride?

"The riders are more relaxed in that environment than in any other," he explained later. "When they're on their bikes, they'll talk about things sometimes they won't talk about in a one-on-one interview or in a group situation. Plus, it lets them know we know what they're doing. Not policeman style but from a point of view of 'Hey, these guys are out here sweating with us.'"

Up through the town of Castagneto Carducci, perched high on a hill, went the team, the riders staying in double file. Once or twice, they swung around a slow-moving tractor or moved tighter to the right to let one of the infrequent cars pass them. The terrain, the riders said, was very much like that in California at their previous camp: gently rolling hills, rarely more than fourth-category climbs.

How did they know which roads to follow?

"Andy's been around here for a while and he knows some of the back roads," Ochowicz said. Hampsten has trained in the area for years and found the hotel, became friends with the family that runs it, and recommended it to the team when it sought a new training site. Jokingly, Hampsten later denied that he guided the training rides. Asked how the team found its way around the hills and then back home, he said, "Just lucky."

Ochowicz set that straight. "Really, these guys are pretty quick to pick up the local roads," he said. "They have a map, too. They find their way around and remember the roads — you do that wherever you train. Don't forget that we train in a lot of countries before and after races. We go to Belgium for a classic and train alongside the canals, they go left and right, and everybody gets a sense for the area pretty quickly."

As the road continued to rise, Ochowicz was dropped and had to hold onto the team car and be towed along behind the riders. ("Some lactic-acid buildup in my arm," he joked later.) Then it was Kuiper's turn to fall back and he pedaled behind the car, enjoying a big draft. Ahead of the team officials and the trailing car, the riders were climbing at a steady 35 kph, a speed that rose to 50 kph when they hit a descent.

Past the green fields of Tuscany and through its villages, looking oddly domestic with wash drying on lines in the intermittent sun, went the team. Traffic was indeed sparse and courteous.

Although the riders were talking and joking as they rolled along, for Alvis, there was time to think.

"I talked with Och' about my program a couple of days ago," he said earlier. "The first big goal for the team, which is where I place my goals, is Milan-San Remo, so my first big goal is to help Lance or whoever else is in contention to win Milan-San Remo.

"It helps to have in my mind where I'm going, so I think of the long-term goals. We might be on a long climb in training, we have the whole team there, and I start thinking about maybe one of the big climbs in the Giro. Or when I'm out alone, doing my intervals, I'm thinking about myself going off the front in the last two kilometers of a race."

After nearly two hours, Jan Schur, who once rode on the formidable East German national team, took a left fork while the rest took a right. "Schur went off to do hill tempos," Ochowicz explained. "It's good to have them all together at least part of the time, but there are different programs for different players." Similarly, the handful of riders who had competed the week before in the Ruta Mexico came back after four hours on the road, while the rest stayed out nearly seven hours.

Ochowicz was asked if a rider ever shirked his training and, if he did, how team officials would know.

"You'd know in three weeks at the races," he replied. "Also, Max Testa does VO_2 testing and you'd see a lack of progress. Then the riders turn in monthly signed training logs, so we can monitor them that way."

The program sounded highly organized.

"It's a business," Ochowicz quickly said.

3 Along the Canal

UNPACKING THE SATCHEL FULL OF TORTILLAS, ALL 1200 OF THEM, Greg LeMond was jubilant. "They're very natural, very good for you," he insisted. "Low fat, just corn and water."

LeMond's love of Mexican food — "some of the best in the world," he says — is well known. "I'll tell you, Mexican food is a lot healthier than the average French food, especially what we get during a race," he continued, stacking packs of tortillas on the counter in his kitchen in Belgium. "Very high fat," he continued in his analysis of what he and his GAN teammates are usually served. "Pasta soaked in butter, vegetables coated in butter and pan-fried steak. Chicken-fried steak." He shuddered. Then he broke into a grin when he found, deep in the satchel, two plastic bags full of green peppers. "Chile rellenos," he announced.

The tortillas came from California because the price was right. "You can buy a five-dozen pack for about $1.50 there, so anytime somebody's coming from California, Otto's son or daughter buys them for us," he said, referring to Otto Jácome, his masseur, trainer and confidant, who lives in the off-season with his family in San Jose, California. At that moment, Jácome's wife, Estella, who was visiting him, was standing at the LeMond family stove and frying pieces of tortilla. As the chips came out of the hot oil, LeMond dunked them in spicy salsa and wolfed them down.

"You don't have to be so strict that you think of food as an evil thing," he said, sounding a mite self-defensive. "Moderation is the key. I'll bet I eat healthier at home than any other rider on the team." He proved that an hour later at dinner: chicken grilled by his wife Kathy on an outdoor barbecue, baked potatoes, and salad with oil-and-vinegar dressing. Dessert was chocolate brownies — and he took just one.

LeMond had a right to be hungry. That afternoon in 1993, he had ridden 208 kilometers in the Grand Prix E3, finishing the minor Belgian race back in the pack, but finishing nevertheless. The next day, he would ride the equally un-important Flèche Brabançonne and again finish its 185 kilometers. For a man who had to spend nearly all of March training rather than racing, his season was finally beginning.

Driving through the flat Belgian countryside later, Jácome nodded to his right where a barge canal ran dark and straight to the horizon. "That's where we work," Jácome said. "You come looking for us, the canal is where you find us."

"Us" was Jácome on a Vespa motor scooter and LeMond just behind him on a bicycle. For a month they traveled the narrow road alongside the canal for as many as 220 kilometers, three or four times a week. Four kermesses, basically exhibition races, helped break the routine. "We did back-to-back days," Jácome said. "Race and train, train and train. He might do 80 kilometers in the morning and then race in the afternoon." For a month, Jácome turned the speed higher, bit by bit, and LeMond pushed that much harder on the pedals to stay right behind him.

"When we started the motorpacing, Greg could do 65, 70 kilometers an hour for three, four, five kilometers," Jácome said. "Then one day, he was doing 80 and then 82. And that was as good as he's ever done, as good as he did when he was win-ning the Tour de France."

The Tour de France is never far from Jácome's mind because it is never far from LeMond's. As his most trusted helper, Jácome has been with LeMond full time since 1988, the year before he overcame a 50-second deficit on the last day of the Tour to win by eight seconds and complete his comeback from the hunting accident that nearly killed him two years earlier.

That winter, LeMond was working toward another comeback, perhaps an even more improbable one. Since his victories in the 1989 and 1990 Tours de France, he had not come close: In 1991, he struggled in the Pyrénées and finished a distant seventh. In 1992, when he had to quit, a victim of exhaustion, midway through the second stage in the Alps, LeMond was dropping out of the Tour for the first time since his debut in the race in 1984. He was barely 23 years old then, raw and vulnerable, an American in a European sport, but already the world professional road race champion. Although he went on to win another world championship and the Tour de France three times, LeMond had not finished first in a race since 1990, except for the 1992 Tour DuPont.

He knew what people were saying.

"I think people have discounted me as a potential winner of the Tour," he admitted.

Did that bother him? "No," he said quickly. "Yeah," he said in the next moment, "it does bother me.

"I don't climb like I used to climb, there's no doubt about that," he said. "My climbing has suffered from weight gains, just being older. But when you get older, other things become more important in your life. Cycling is not the No. 1 priority to a cyclist who has a wife and kids. It's hard for people to understand that my family is my No. 1 priority, my family and my health. I've always chosen that way and if people don't like it, they don't have to hire me.

"I've been criticized for it, but I feel I've made the right choice. This is the way it is.

"Cycling is not a sport like basketball or baseball, where you can do it on natural talent. You don't have to work out in those sports five or six hours a day. Cycling is more like Olympic gymnastics, where you train and train and your career lasts eight years.

"But here your career lasts longer. You might spend four or five years as an amateur, just getting to the level where your can turn pro, and then four years to the level where you can do well — nine or 10 years before you start producing in cycling. If you want to really make money, you have to keep producing six or seven more years.

"So you're talking 15, 16, 17 years and it's almost impossible to live that long like a monk. There are some cyclists who can, but I'm not one of them. I'm not capable of that kind of life. The way I've done my career has always been my maximum for me to be happy. I've tried to balance everything to where I've gotten my maximum athletic performance, but I've also been happy doing what I was doing.

"I might have been able to improve my performances through a strict vegetarian diet, for instance, or a strict diet through the winter, but for me that's like spending three months in hell. I enjoy the winter and it's my time to let loose."

LeMond was in a chatty mood as he drove from his home in Kortrijk to

Brussels for the insignificant Flèche Brabançonne race. Despite the pressures on him to succeed, he looked and sounded relaxed as he reminisced about his many years in the sport, starting as a teenager in Nevada.

"When I was just about 17 years old, in 1978, I sat down in my room in our house in Washoe Valley, Nevada, with a yellow writing pad, the kind with lines on it, and wrote down my goals, my career goals, the way I wanted my life to go," he once recalled.

"I wanted to accomplish 'x' amount by the time I was 24 or 25. What I didn't want was to be the kind of cyclist who just stuck it out, stayed in the sport for 10 years without being successful. So I sat down before the junior world championships and wrote for 1978 'Place well, for experience, in junior world championships.' And I wrote that in 1979 I want to win the junior world's. The following year I want to win the Olympic road race, by the time I'm 22 or 23, I want to win the professional world championship and by the time I'm 24 or 25 I want to win the Tour de France.

"I actually wrote this down — I don't know where the list is now but I think I still have it somewhere in my old bedroom. I was almost 17 years old and I was determined that this was the way I wanted my career to go.

"And that's the way it went. Everything that was on that paper I did except for the Olympics, and that was boycotted by the United States."

He was remembering now that, as a young fan of professional racing, he read about the Tour de France and the major classics in fan magazines imported from Europe.

"Paris-Roubaix and the Tour of Flanders were the races I saw in pictures and read about," he said. "I always had this idea I'd like to do well in them. When you're young, a first-year pro, you think you can win anything," LeMond added with a sigh. "I've come close, I've been there, but I haven't pulled it off yet." He fell silent and only the sound of the engine filled the car.

Then he started again: "I had a very bad winter in terms of stress," he said, turning silent again. Grimacing, he regarded a frontier and decided to cross it. My father, he started.

LeMond told it quickly: Just before Thanksgiving, he traveled to Reno, Nevada, to fire his father as head of the family bicycle business, LeMond Enterprises, Inc., in California. Bob LeMond had run up more than $1 million in debts. There was more to it than that, his son continued. The company was badly run and Bob LeMond was not the person to be its president. Greg LeMond had told him that.

Then he spent weeks reorganizing the company. The money that was gone, LeMond continued, was money he had earned and earmarked for his retirement.

He and his parents had not spoken in months. They would not return his infrequent calls. My mother, he said, she won't ever forgive me. She'll probably never talk to me again. My father, he said, maybe someday we'll be close again. Maybe not.

He had not been sleeping well, LeMond continued. "Thank God for Kathy," he exclaimed. "Without her, I think I would have gone crazy over the winter."

A long silence followed.

Perhaps he was thinking about how things used to be, before the breakup with his parents....

❀

AFTER THE USUAL POST-TOUR DE FRANCE NIGHT ON THE TOWN IN Paris, in 1991, the riders and their entourages began to disperse. For Greg LeMond and his support group, that was no easy task.

He was traveling to west France to ride in a couple of criteriums, or exhibition races, while his wife Kathy and their oldest son Geoffrey were going home to Belgium to pick up the two other LeMond children, Scott and Simone. Later in the week they all planned to fly home to Minnesota.

As for the rest of LeMond's Tour de France party, his parents Bob and Bertha LeMond flew home to Nevada once the race ended, taking with them Art LeMond, Greg's grandfather, and Randy Rupracht, the Nevada teenager with cystic fibrosis who was Greg's guest on the Tour for the second successive year. Kathy LeMond's parents, Sacia and Dr. David Morris, flew to Wisconsin. Dick and Frieda Lauer, the couple who sold Greg and Kathy LeMond their home in Minnesota and then became close friends, flew to Minnesota. Lisa and Tim Morris, Kathy LeMond's brother- and sister-in-law, headed for Chicago. Fred Mengoni, Greg's longtime friend and adviser, went home to New York.

"Oh gosh, are there more?" asked Bertha LeMond while she was counting off the people who spent all or most of the three-week race with her son. Yes, there were more. Pat and Joyce Morrisey, the senior LeMonds' friends "who've know Greg since he was a boy" also headed back to Nevada.

"We're a close family," Bob LeMond said during the race. He described his relationship with his son as "very good," adding that "we talk a lot."

This closeness and the fact that so many members of his family traveled with the rider enchanted European fans, who knew that bicycle racing was usually a reclusive sport. Most riders' wives and children appear only on a day off in a long race, not at nearly every stage. Even the French press, often resistant to change, was sympathetic when Kathy LeMond missed her husband's strong third-place finish in the prologue in Lyon because she had taken all three children to the local zoo.

Aside from Greg LeMond, who slept in the team hotel during the race, the family needed from 9 to 12 rooms a night. The family used four cars, including a van, for transport.

"We do it for our sake as much as for Greg's," explained Bertha LeMond. "We don't get to see him much otherwise. Kathy has seen him only 25 days so far this year away from races." Since she dislikes being interviewed, Bob LeMond carried on for his wife from there. He spoke as the father of the rider trying and failing to win his third successive Tour de France and his fourth in all. At the finish, LeMond was seventh overall.

"If he doesn't win, it really doesn't matter to us at all," said Bob LeMond, formerly a real estate broker in Reno and, at that time, his son's business manager. "This is a bike race. There are many other things in life that are so much more important and so much more of humanity's concern.

"It's important to his career," he continued, "to his immediate self-feeling, but in the overall picture it isn't that important." As he spoke, his son remained in his hotel room, busy giving and trying to fend off interviews.

"It's a continuous barrage of people that want something, a lot of sincere, good requests," Bob LeMond said. "Sometimes he gets a little stressed out with me over my trying to manage things, handle all the calls. I try to say no as much as possible. It's difficult, but Greg's time is so limited."

Yet he noted ruefully that his son has a reputation for not being able to say no. Greg LeMond rarely turns away an autograph seeker and is sometimes late to sign in at races because people along the way want to chat. "He's conscious of people's feelings," his father said. "I'm proud of that sensitivity of his.

"I'm proud of all my kids." The LeMonds also have two daughters, Kathy and Karen.

"The most important thing is teaching your kids from when they're babies that they've got to play by the rules, and to live with rules and morality in your life. We had strict rules about where you were, when you had to be home. It was cut and dried."

Cutting off allowances was not an option, since LeMond said his children had not received them. Instead, discipline was enforced by "not going out any more, or whatever was necessary." Mostly, he said, he believed in positive reinforcement. "You've got to teach self-confidence: no criticism when they're young. We've never found fault with our kids. We may have chastised them but we never criticized them … and I think they're very confident."

LeMond linked his son's self-confidence to "his desire to win."

"I'm awed by it," he revealed, "that determination to succeed at what he set out to do. He's unbelievable. If he never wins another Tour de France, he's already won three plus two world championships, so who really cares? He's one of the most well-known athletes in the world, a household name in Australia or Japan or Colombia.

"Greg LeMond, my son, I think he has achieved more than almost any rider in the history of the sport. Greg has brought everything to modern-day cycling. He's changed it completely, starting with salaries."

LeMond noted that most teams now wear jerseys with zippers down the full front to help cool riders as they climb. Until a few years earlier, standard jerseys had only a small zipper, just enough of an opening to pull the garment on.

"The longer zipper? That was Greg," his father said. "Sunglasses, helmets, he's changed everything. Incomes to riders, income to teams, he's made this a world sport. His accomplishments are far beyond whether he wins this Tour de France."

❀

ARRIVING AT THE SPORTS CENTER IN BRUSSELS WHERE THE FLÈCHE Brabançonne was to begin, Greg LeMond parked the car … and immediately put thoughts of his personal problems behind him. "You need racing," he said. "You need it to get yourself in better shape. You can test yourself, see where you're at, judge yourself. I want to do well today, test myself.

"And I like racing," he was saying as he left the car and began signing autographs, moving slowly but decisively toward the team bus that held his bicycle. "After all these years, racing's still exciting."

4 Back to Where He Was

THE DAY BEFORE THE 1994 PARIS-ROUBAIX RACE IN APRIL, GREG LEMOND hoped to get an answer to the question of how far back he had come. "I'm feeling okay," he said brightly as teams filed into a civic center for a presentation on national television. Paris-Roubaix, the classic race also known as the Hell of the North, is that big a race.

"We'll see tomorrow," LeMond continued. "My condition was a lot better in January than it's been now. I was training very well, but when I came back to Europe in February, I got the flu for a week and that took me off my bike for nearly two weeks." Earlier in his career, when recovery was not so difficult, he judged that each week off the bicycle called for two weeks of training to return to the same level. Now that time seemed to be increasing. "I didn't get back to my same level until the end of March," he said. "It was almost a two-month stagnation period."

How had his training gone in San Diego? "It was good, I was training well, I had good weather." He pulled at the zipper of his heavy jacket: April in Paris, even April in Compiègne — a small city about 50 miles northeast of Paris and the start of the Paris-Roubaix race — is usually cold and rainy, no matter what the song says. "I can't wait to get out of this weather," LeMond said.

He would be leaving Europe in a few days to return to the United States. First, he planned to visit his family for two or three days and then would go training in

Northern California or, more likely, North Carolina, wherever the weather was better. Like most riders, he detested races in the cold and rain, the usual conditions for the spring classics.

"To spend the next two weeks in Belgium in the rain and the cold, you don't get that far," he said. "And even if I stay, there are only two races — the Amstel Gold Race and Liège-Bastogne-Liège — and I'm not at the level for them. Too hilly. I'm okay for a flat race like Paris-Roubaix, but the others are a bit above my ability now." The Tour of Flanders a week before had proven that. "I was tired," he admitted. "My legs were dead. I'm doing okay, but I expected to be a little bit better right now than I am. If only I could have continued the same progression through February, I'd be quite a bit better. But I got sick."

Along with his GAN team, LeMond was summoned then to a television session. His new trainer, Adrie Van Diemen, a Dutchman, stayed behind and continued the discussion.

"I think he's not so bad, he's coming up," Van Diemen said of LeMond. "But he's too sensitive to cold weather and can't perform in it." Van Diemen said he was emphasizing recuperation periods for his rider. "He has extraordinary potential for big races, but he can easily overtrain. He must recuperate every time before he starts a new race. The best way to do that is to say you should skip a race because you're getting too fatigued, but you have sponsors to satisfy. They don't like you to skip races."

No, they don't — especially when they are paying a rider more than $500,000 a year with bonus clauses for winning a big race like, say, Paris-Roubaix. So, on a cold and drizzly morning, LeMond began Paris-Roubaix. He lasted about halfway, seeming to go down in a crash and disappear in the cobblestone stretch of the Arenberg Forest. It was worse than that, he said later.

"I flatted, not crashed. In the long cobblestone section before the Arenberg, I flatted. Nobody was there to give me a wheel and I rode four or five kilometers on a flat tire. Finally I changed it, came back with two kilometers to go to the Arenberg, entered it in about 10th position in the second group. Everybody crashed in front of me and I came through solo and could see the first group there, 15 seconds in front of me, and I was feeling great, I wasn't slipping, I was real stable on that mud.

"I felt really good and I was starting to pour on the pressure when ... pssssh ... I flat my rear tire. I kept riding and my teammates passed me because they didn't see I had a flat tire since I was moving. I knew there was no team car behind me with wheels, so I kept riding, riding, riding. But you can't ride on a flat tire through the Forest of Arenberg. Everybody in that second group that crashed passed me.

"When finally I changed my wheel I came out of the Arenberg at least three, four minutes behind. I lost so much time. The next cobblestone section I crashed and thought I broke my elbow." That was it for him.

⊛

FRAMED ON THE WALL, A *MIROIR-SPRINT* MAGAZINE COVER SHOWED a tight-faced Eddy Merckx pedaling through the rain, alone except for his motor-cycle escort. A *L'Équipe* special edition portrayed Roger De Vlaeminck pulling away in heavy gloom from his closest chaser. From the cover of *Sport Club*, Fausto Coppi stared defiantly, only his forehead white where his cap had kept the dust off. Another issue of *L'Équipe* showed Greg LeMond trying to smile, minstrel-like, through a mask of mud.

Pausing now and again to sign an autograph, Rolf Sørensen was admiring the Paris-Roubaix art show a day before the race itself. Sørensen — a Danish rider on the Italian team Ariostea, and a wearer of the yellow jersey in the 1991 Tour de France — had stepped back into his youth. "I was five, six, seven years old when I became a fan. That's the way I started: looking at pictures. Eddy Merckx ... everybody. My favorite riders were Merckx, of course, De Vlaeminck ... all the big riders."

Two decades later, his favorites had barely changed. "I still have Merckx as an idol, De Vlaeminck, Francesco Moser. Also Hinault. He's the last, I feel the last, really big, big rider who won everything."

Sørensen had stopped at a booth with a display of Bernard Hinault photographs, mostly from the Tour de France. Hinault did not like the Paris-Roubaix race, the Hell of the North, and stopped riding it as soon as he won it in 1981.

"It's a special race," Sørensen said of the century-old Paris-Roubaix, where cobblestones cover a fifth of its 267.5 kilometers (166 miles). When the weather's wet, the cobbles are treacherously slippery; when it's dry, dust from the road chokes the riders. In any weather, the cobblestones leave the riders' bodies, especially their arms and hands, beaten and weary.

Some riders consistently do well in Paris-Roubaix. Merckx won the race three times, as did the Italian Moser and Belgian star Rik Van Looy. Roger De Vlaeminck won it a record four times.

Dutchman Hennie Kuiper won it just once, in 1983, but as he proudly noted, "I rode Paris-Roubaix 14 times and was in the top 10 seven times. I have all the places, including the most important — I won it. In my living room, there are no photographs from my career but there is a big cobblestone. It's the trophy they give to the winner. And every morning when I wake up, that big cobblestone looks at me."

The Dutchman now is the directeur sportif of the Motorola team and so shares his secrets about how to do well in the race. "You must wait until the last two sections of cobblestones," he said. "You must not attack too early, you must keep feeding and drinking — it's 270 k's, on the cobblestones and you burn a lot of energy. Sometimes when you're too concentrated and nervous, you forget that. But the real secret is good legs."

Kuiper had them in 1983 when he fell twice and recovered each time to get back quickly with the lead attacking group. Sixteen kilometers from the finish, he went off alone, building a lead of one minute 30 seconds. Then he rolled into one of the many potholes that lace the many cobbles.

"I broke my rim," he remembered, "so I had to wait for the team car. Seconds are like hours then. When you wait and can do nothing, you go crazy." The mild-tempered Kuiper screamed with rage as he waited for a new bicycle. "By the time the car came, Madiot, Moser and Duclos-Lassalle were right behind me and I got another bike with only a few seconds' lead." It was enough. When the race finished on the track at Roubaix, Kuiper was 1:15 ahead of Gilbert Duclos-Lassalle, in second place.

"Second again," Duclos wailed. In 1980, when he was in just his third year as a professional, he finished second to Moser in Paris-Roubaix. That was the last of the Italian's three successive victories; he was 29 years old and at the crest of a glorious career on the road.

For Duclos, just 25, it was only a beginning. Earlier that season, after he won the Tour of Corsica, Paris-Nice and the Tour du Tarn, he was widely proclaimed as the next great French rider. That was a judgment the two second places in Paris-Roubaix seemed to confirm ... and a major victory looked to be not far off.

But by 1992, Duclos was still waiting. In the nine intervening years, he had an honorable career, winning his share of small races, but never a really big one. Among his 60 victories were sprinkled such names as the Midi Libre, the Tour of Sweden, the Grand Prix of Plouay and Bordeaux-Paris. Since his lamented second place, the closest he had come to victory in Paris-Roubaix was fourth in 1989.

Duclos-Lassalle would be 38 years old that August and had become one of the oldest professionals in the sport. Time saps ambition and corrodes skill. Yes,

Duclos had lost much of his youthful swagger. He had surmounted a hunting accident in which he nearly destroyed his left hand and had borne the change in status from team leader to road captain — the honorary rank accorded to veterans because they have been there before. Winners are never road captains.

But road captains, as Duclos showed, are sometimes winners.

Coming out of the Arenberg Forest, a 2.4-kilometer trench of ancient cobblestones and rutted shoulders, he worked himself toward the front of the pack. He remembered, he said later, that Moser attacked at this very spot far back in 1980. Moser believed in shattering the pack with sudden accelerations that left his rivals heavy in the legs and without conviction that they could catch him.

Off went Duclos-Lassalle. By Kuiper's standards, he attacked far too early, but Paris-Roubaix has no rules except that nobody wins by remaining passive. A couple of others joined Duclos and they began to overtake the early leaders, shedding some, keeping others. Within 40 kilometers, Duclos and three companions had a clear road ahead to Roubaix, 70 kilometers away. A flat reduced the group to three and then, with 46 kilometers to go, Duclos sped away alone, nearly two minutes ahead of the pack.

His lead gradually came down but he never was caught. Too many chasers watched each other and waited for somebody else to make the first move. Occasionally, somebody did and members of Duclos's team, especially Greg LeMond, caught and neutralized them. For the first time in 1992, LeMond was in wonderful form, peaking for the one classic that motivates him. Yet he played the team game, working for the teammate in front, refusing to attack himself, chasing down rivals, slowing the chase by staying at the front.

Over the seasons, Duclos-Lassalle had not won big races, but he had influenced a few. Two years earlier, when LeMond might have lost the Tour de France because of a flat tire in the Pyrénées, Duclos was far ahead and hoping to win the stage. Instead he obeyed orders, stopped, waited for his team leader and helped him storm back to the front. LeMond was thanking him again.

With 17 kilometers to go in the 1992 Paris-Roubaix, Olaf Ludwig of the Panasonic team broke free and tried to overhaul Duclos-Lassalle. With 14 kilometers to go, Ludwig narrowed the lead to 50 seconds. With eight kilometers to go, it was 38 seconds, with five kilometers to go, 32 seconds, with four kilometers to go, 28 seconds. Ludwig had waited too long.

Ludwig was a lap behind as Duclos-Lassalle sailed around the 400-meter track at the Roubaix Velodrome before crossing the finish line. Both his arms were upright in a victory salute, both his fists were clenched, and through the dust of Paris-

Roubaix on his face, he was wearing a smile that, for a man nearly 38 years old, could be called boyish.

5 Showing the Jersey

LANCE ARMSTRONG WAS SURROUNDED BY TEAM OFFICIALS AND TEAM-mates happy to give him guidance; so why did he listen to nobody in his zeal to do well in the 1994 Milan-San Remo race? Or why did nobody point out that Armstrong was overdoing it? All through March, in minor stage races in Spain and Italy, Armstrong worked hard at overdoing it: He would finish that day's long race and then go off on his own for another 60 or 80 kilometers. That was the program.

Anybody who remembered him in training camp in Italy — moving out of his seat and nearer the television set whenever a videotape of the previous year's Milan-San Remo was played — would understand. The rest of the Motorola team lounged in the back of the dining hall, maybe looking at the videotape, maybe not, because they had seen it so many times already. Armstrong never had enough of it: He was drawn to each showing of Milan-San Remo and would stand silent as the images of the race flickered by. The descent down the Cipressa, the climb up the Poggio hill, time after time.

To no effect. "Milan-San Remo, that was a failure," he admitted late in the spring. "I give myself an 'F' there." Had he been overtrained? "Yes," he said flatly. "I was tired, rundown, overtrained to a point. Anyway, that was no good," he continued, brushing the race aside and rushing ahead in his review of his performances in the spring classics. The world champion had not gotten off to the impressive start he sought.

"Then Flanders, another failure, the same problem, the same feeling, the same run-down, tired feeling. Then I went to Pays Basque and that's when I started to think it couldn't get any worse. I was feeling so bad. We had a climb and I couldn't elevate my heart rate, and I went straight to the back.

"After three or four days, I stopped and went home to my Italian base in Como, and said to myself, 'This is the bottom. It can't get any worse than this. I have to start turning this around.' So I rested, just rested and rested. I rested a lot. I had rested before Flanders also, but it wasn't enough. After I quit Pays Basque, I rested for at least a week." By then, it was generally understood that Armstrong had done too much over the winter and compounded the excessive roadwork by his heavy schedule early in the spring in Mexico, Italy and Spain. "I was in too good condition in February," he said. The long rest in Italy began to help him recover.

"I rode, but very minimal, saw the doctor a lot and was feeling better ... and things started to come around. I had some personal problems, too, that I straightened out," he continued, referring to a former girlfriend who could not adapt to the move from Texas to Italy. For all his worldliness and even suavity — a word not often applied to Armstrong, but accurate — he was still just 22 years old, not that long removed from the turmoil and torments of a teenager. As he spoke, as he speaks, he reminded an older man of his own youth and his own children.

"Another thing is, I changed my position on my bike," he went on. "Last year, I rode one position and then I went to a steeper position and then, just before Liège-Bastogne-Liège, I went back to the old position and the same bike I rode at the world championships. So I straightened out the personal problems, straightened out the position problems, and things started to come around. Got my mom over ... so three things at once."

Results started to come in the classics: second place in Liège-Bastogne-Liège, 13th in the Amstel Gold Race. "Liège was a success, that was a nice one — 'A minus.' In Liège, I was coming back from the bottom, so for me to get second, I was really happy. Amstel I felt good. I would grade it on how I felt so I would give it an 'A.'

"Overall," he summed up, "it was an average spring."

Now that his results were better, Armstrong realized he had a lot to be pleased about. One was how much easier he found living in Europe in his second year there. "Europe is not such a strange place anymore. It's becoming more and more like home, which is a relief, because I can't spend how many years of my career being miserable over there. So now it's more and more comfortable.

"I don't mind Europe very much," he decided.

In addition to working out the traditional problem of being an American racer in Europe, far from home and a familiar culture, he was learning more about who he was and who he hoped to become.

Armstrong draws a distinction between being and having a personality. "I just want to win bike races, be a bike racer, not a personality," he stated. "But you can be a bike racer and still have personality."

After he dropped out of the 1993 Tour de France, Armstrong returned home to Italy to recover, while the race completed its clockwise swing through France and the finish in Paris. On the next-to-last day, he rejoined the race as a spectator at the final time trial. The real reason, he confided, was that he did not want to miss the Motorola team's traditional celebration party at a Tex-Mex restaurant in Paris. "A Texas boy like me wouldn't miss a time like that," he said.

Looking fit and relaxed at the time trial's start south of Paris, Armstrong summed up that year's Tour with a tribute to Miguel Indurain: "I tell you, it would be a great race if he wasn't in it. It would be much more exciting without him. It might even be better for the sport — a serious, serious race. But you can't blame the guy for that. He dominates.

"He's definitely the best bike racer around. I look at him as the ultimate."

Then he paid a meaningful personal compliment to the Spanish champion: "If I came close to idolizing anybody, it would be Indurain. I'd love to ride with a guy like that. Had we not gotten the renewal, I would have loved being on his team next year." Armstrong referred to Motorola's agreement to continue sponsoring the team for another year.

"He's got a super attitude," Armstrong continued. "He's not obnoxious, he's quiet, he respects the other riders, he never fusses. He's so mild-mannered. I really like him."

So much so that the Spaniard seemed to have become a role model for Armstrong, who confessed, "I still have a temper and an attitude sometimes.

"I wouldn't mind molding myself into his sort of character," he concluded. "Really quiet, just goes about his business."

❋

LIVING IN AUSTIN, TEXAS, J.T. NEAL WAS PLANNING TO WORK AS A

masseur for the Subaru-Montgomery team during the Tour of Texas in 1990. Eddie Borysewicz, the team's directeur sportif, told Neal, "I have a new rider and I want you to meet him, maybe he might need some work before the race." The rider was Lance Armstrong, who was living then in Plano, Texas.

Neal continues the story: "He came and I gave him a massage that afternoon before the race, and he liked my work, and he said he was planning to move to Austin anyway at a given time … and I happened to have an apartment that adjoins my studio in downtown Austin, centrally located near the university. And I said, 'Well, it will be available probably at that time, whenever.' So we worked out the dates — the girl living in there was moving out — and it ended up that he moved in. And I started working massage on him at that time."

While he remained Armstrong's masseur and landlord, Neal's relationship with the new rider on the Subaru team broadened. Did Armstrong consider Neal something of a surrogate father? "Uh huh, yeah," he agreed. Did Neal consider Armstrong something of a surrogate son? "Of course."

"I feel it's a very close relationship," Neal said. "I'm able to say whatever I feel, and he's able to talk to me and I give him advice, just like I would to a son." With two daughters and a son ("They're all younger than Lance, and he's sort of like a big brother"), Neal has experience in the paternal line. "Just like your children, you tell Lance what you think … and he's going to do what he wants to do anyway," he joked.

His view of Armstrong is tender: "Lance has always been a little bit more mature in a lot of ways than a normal person. I think it was because he was on his own for a long time. He was resilient. He's just more mature — not in every way, but in many ways. He's very warm.

"He's also frugal. The only thing he did after he won the world's is, he bought a car, a Japanese sports car. But that's the only thing he's done. He's generous but very frugal.

"One of his other qualities is, he's very patriotic. He's just everything USA and very sincere about it. He really gets turned on. I remember him telling me that when he won the Thrift Drug Classic in Pittsburgh as an amateur — this was prior to the Olympics — how the people were atop that hard hill, hollering U-S-A, U-S-A, and that just kept him going great, so happy."

After that 1990 Tour of Texas, Neal began working also for the U.S. national team, with which Armstrong then rode, too. Neal still looks after Armstrong in U.S. races, but not in Europe, where he is not part of the Motorola team's program. "But I did go to Europe and picked him up when he got out of the Tour de France,"

Neal said. "I took him back to Como and worked on him for the whole time, to get him ready for the world's. I did massage, worked on him every day for an hour, an hour and a half. He was in deteriorated shape — the Tour takes a lot out of you and he needed a lot of work.

"A lot of new, different things, and I didn't even have a massage table. I had to work with him on the dining room table — that's all I had at his apartment." Neal and his wife, who accompanied him during part of his stay, did not get to see much of the 1993 Tour, visiting the race only for the last two days when Armstrong returned for the farewell party. "And then we went back to Como, and I worked with him four more days," the masseur said.

Neal came by his trade in a roundabout way. A native of Alabama, he went to law school in Texas although, as he put it, "I don't do much law any more.

"I was doing real estate law and the real estate market fell apart. Especially in Texas when the price of oil went from $30 a barrel to $10 and they changed the tax laws on owning real estate. I decided I would do a new career until the market got better. So I went to massage school and started working with swimmers." Whether the market has improved or not, Neal stays with massage.

He planned to go to Italy during the Tour de France again in 1994, but not follow the race. "Motorola already has their group and I would be like an outsider," he felt. "But in case Lance drops out like last year, then I'll be in Como, waiting on him. Getting ready for the world's. I'm bringing my wife and one of my daughters to Italy and we'll stay at Lance's apartment. I think it's important that I work on him after the Tour. For recovery."

As the man who kneads the body, Neal has no complaints with Armstrong's eating habits. "He eats well," he said. "He has his favorite restaurants in Austin and he won't eat junk food. He doesn't think it's good for you. He likes to eat high carbohydrates. There's a mostly organic health food store in Austin and it's only four blocks from the house, so he shops there and sometimes he does a lot of his own cooking. The main thing is, he eats carefully. Lance loves Mexican food but not spicy, not real hot and spicy. Tex-Mex. He's not a jalapeno type. Burritos."

6 Back in America

"YOU THINK YOU HAVE A LOT OF TIME BETWEEN THESE RACES — and you really don't," Greg LeMond was saying in Wilmington, Delaware, a day before the 1994 Tour DuPont began in May. He detailed how he had spent the month between Paris-Roubaix and the DuPont: "I went home for a week, and then I went for training to Asheville, North Carolina." He liked the sound of the name and tried it again, drawing it out with a Dixie accent: "Asheville, North Carolina." Feeling frisky, he tacked on "Nashville, Tennessee." LeMond was definitely relaxed. "Asheville, North Carolina, Nashville, Tennessee," he drawled.

"I really felt flat for about 10 days when I got home," he continued. "I just didn't feel —" A yawn. "I stayed in Minnesota for a little longer because the weather was so nice; it got up into the 80s there." He had done some training — three or four days — but not much, he admitted, because his left knee hurt a bit after his crash in Paris-Roubaix. That knee bore a fair-sized scab.

"Then I went down to Asheville. It's gorgeous training down there — hilly, mountainous — and I had maybe 10 good days of it. One day, I did a nine-hour ride,

I was out way longer than I planned. I did a lot of good climbing, just riding in warm weather, 80 to 85 degrees every day. A good time."

It had been a solitary time, too, since his family could not accompany him. The children were in school. But it hadn't been lonely. "Usually when I'm home and training, there are so many people around; so it's nice to be isolated." Why Asheville? "Because the race is going there and I'd heard it was pretty nice and they had decent climbs down there and the weather — I looked at the Weather Channel and it was always at least in the 70s there. California, I can count on it — but this race is on the East Coast, and from the West Coast to the East is three hours, a big time change. And I wanted to go someplace different. I'd never been to the South. I liked it. The training was much better than California. Unbelievable."

The weekend between the end of training and the start of the DuPont he had done well in the First Union Grand Prix in Atlanta, finishing fourth in the field sprint, which didn't hurt his mood either.

"I was riding pretty good," he agreed. "I broke a wheel at the crucial moment when the breakaway went away, had no team car, changed my wheel, and I was at least a minute by myself chasing the group that was going superfast. I was at my max when I caught the group. It took me two laps to recuperate and the break was already gone. Once I recuperated, I did a lot of work to pull back some of the guys in front, but there were still four guys away.

"I felt good that day. I tried to get away with a 'k' to go, I put out a lot of effort then. It's a good sign when you put out a lot of effort and you still feel good at the end, you're able to sprint."

This all was prelude. Time for the big question: Had he any idea of how well he would climb in the DuPont?

"No, I don't," he answered. "I'm always worried now about the hills. I don't climb like I used to, mainly because I'm a little heavier in my maturity. That's my only question: climbing. Even when I was younger and at my best, I could climb with anybody; but I could never drop anybody on a climb. I always made my time up in time trials."

He weighed, he said, 72 kilograms, or 158 pounds. "I'm at 9-percent body fat and I figure I can drop 3 kilos and be at 4-percent body fat. At 3 kilos lighter, I'll fly up hills. Or at least stay with any rider. I still have a couple of kilos to go," the same four or five pounds he had to go for the last several years. LeMond was not being overly reassuring about his condition if he had to fall back on his difficulty in losing a bit of weight. Then he zeroed in on his goals.

"What I hope is to find that I'm very close to the best riders here. I still have a lot of improvement to make between here and, say, the Tour de France." He dropped the Tour's name diffidently, just one of many arbitrary reference points, he would have liked to imply — as if he might have said "between here and, say, the Dauphiné Libéré" or "between here and, say, the Tour of Switzerland."

"I think I'll make a lot of improvement here," LeMond went on hurriedly, covering his mock naïveté. Just the Tour de France, the only race that motivated him.

Exactly where, on a scale to 100, did he rate himself this morning in May? "Maybe 80 percent," he said softly. Then his voice grew louder, more buoyant. "I'm feeling okay," he insisted. "I'm feeling like things are finally coming around. I had a stagnation period, just wasn't feeling great, back in March and April. I mean I felt *good*" — he underlined the word — "but not like I felt in January when I was feeling great. I felt unbelievable then.

"I got my power output on my (bicycle) computer and I could see that in March I was not nearly as good as I was in January. Only this month have I come back to that level. Really in those two months, three months you should have made *improvement*" — another underlined word. "That's the way it is.

"Sometimes when you race, you don't make any improvement, because the racing is so hard that you blow yourself out and you have to recover. I felt as if I needed these three weeks out to retrain myself. I wish I could have had another week or two. You don't get better if you don't recuperate."

Recuperation and LeMond's diminishing ability to recover quickly had been major worries the last few years. Not since 1990, when he was chasing Claudio Chiappucci in the Tour de France and was startlingly relaxed about the Italian's big lead, had LeMond been able to boast that he was at his best in the last week of the three-week race.

Being back in the United States, seeing his family, enjoying the warm weather pleased him enormously. "If I could race this way, I'd race forever. From now to the world's, it's my favorite time of the season. I could race for another couple of years if I never had to go back to Europe in February or March. I could pop over for the (April) classics, for a three-week period, but February and March I'd never miss. I'd rather be in warm weather, training well, than racing, killing yourself, having setbacks, sicknesses, this and that. I'd like to race next year, but I wouldn't like to do it on the same basis as this year.

"My ideal year would be to train well all winter, maybe train in California until the DuPont, maybe do the Tour of Colombia, on this side of the hemisphere, good weather, good conditions, where my morale is always high, and then next year the Tour of Spain, the world's, they go to September and October. So next year I'd like to do the Tour DuPont, go to Italy and do the Tour of Italy, do the Tour de France, come back, do the Tour of Spain, do the world's."

His burst of enthusiasm done, LeMond must have realized that, going on age 33 and in his 14th year as a professional, he had just mapped out the first three-Tour season of his career. Not only his own first but the first for any major rider in many years. "Next year," he said, backing off his grand design, "might not include any of those things.

"Maybe this year, if I have a bad year, I might call it quits. I hope not. I hope not because I'm a better-educated cyclist in the way I prepare, and I hate to have invested all this time and energy in training and have it just for this year. One thing I want to do is have one solid year this year, not have these ups and these crashes. I truly believe that I should have a better year — if I stay motivated — next year because one solid year...." The end of the sentence hung, unspoken.

"I just want to have the Tour de France to the world's where I keep progressing, where I can finish the season fresh, not finish wasted. Not like 1992, '91. The 1991 Tour de France, where I forced myself to finish, wound up getting seventh, it blew me out for the rest of the year. I was just dead. And in '92 I was done for the rest of the season. And it keeps setting you up for a bad season the next year. If I could finish a good season this year, take a little break at the end of the year, restart an early program again, maybe next year I could reach another level."

Another level — there it was again, a frankness in admitting that he had slipped. No talk now of one or two kilos too many limiting him in the mountains or how much better he trained in good weather. And what was this sudden talk of how there might not even be a next year if this year showed no progress? This was not the LeMond who liked to talk about remaining in the sport through 1996 so that he might compete at the Olympic Games in Atlanta. The LeMond speaking now seemed to understand just how vulnerable he was.

"I'm glad to be here racing and being competitive," he continued. "I know it's disappointing for some people to think I can accept just being competitive. When you have a bad year like last year, you're happy just to be back and feeling good. Feeling capable of recovering every day, of racing with good riders.

"And when I'm feeling a little better, I'll take the next step: I'll say, 'Hey, I'm going to really go for this race to win.'

"I might be at that level right now. I might surprise myself."

He was talking easily, almost free-associating, gaining confidence from his words, believing in himself anew. There was nothing false or hollow about his flight because there is nothing false or hollow about LeMond himself: His considerable charm, his open friendliness have always been based on optimism. With LeMond, all things have always been possible, no matter what the handicaps. The first American to become a bicycle racing star in Europe? So many others had failed where he had stuck it out and succeeded. A rider who could be betrayed by his friend, teammate and idol, Bernard Hinault, and still not crack? LeMond passed that test in 1986 and won his first Tour de France. A man who could come back from a nearly fatal shooting and win the Tour de France again, making up a 50-second deficit on the final day? Through the long nights of doubt, he continued to dream. If he wanted to dream now, who would be so uncaring and dare try to stop him?

"I want to enjoy myself here," he said. "I'm in the last stage of my career and I don't want to make every race a life or death thing. Like the years after my hunting accident, every race I went into it was 'If I don't do well here, I'm quitting.' And everybody saying, 'He's not going to come back, look how bad he's riding.' I'm not going to do that. Deep inside, I know that my talent's there and it's just a question of training it back up to where it should be."

He stopped and gazed out the window at the slums of Wilmington that nearly circled the hotel. A feeble sun was shining, but the weather forecast for the prologue that evening was rain and, sure enough, dark clouds were building on the horizon. Metaphorically, too.

"It's easy to say I want to win this race, I feel great, I'm going to kick butt," LeMond continued. "It's easy to say when you're off the bike and talking to journalists. But when reality sits in the bike race, when you find out there are other guys who are just stronger than you...."

"Bicycling is a humbling sport. When you think you've mastered it, you haven't mastered it.

"I've had a lot more setbacks than most riders. When I think of my first six years as a pro, it seems that every year you made a bit of improvement, every year you felt a little better, and then I had this hunting accident and your whole world is turned around. I still can't believe how hard it was to come back, go through all the setbacks."

Did he want to come back as much now as he did after the 1987 shooting?

"Oh I do, I do," he said quickly and perhaps automatically. Then he paused. "In a sense I do," he corrected himself. "I don't think I could handle now the setbacks I had between my hunting accident and winning the Tour in '89. Injuring my tendon, having another surgery — I couldn't handle that now. I'd probably quit.

"I say that now, but you do what you do because you don't have a choice.

"Don't underestimate my desire." he warned. "When I don't feel good, it's hard for me to be positive, say I'm going to win. I've trained more this winter and I've been dedicated, more dedicated than I've ever been in my career."

❄

SOME PROFESSIONAL RIDERS ARE HAPPY TO RETIRE, NEVER CLIMB another mountain, end the long hours of training and the weeks away from home. Bernard Hinault — LeMond's former mentor — is a good example: He said he was retiring on his 32nd birthday in 1986 and retire he did, without a second thought about that elusive sixth victory in the Tour de France. Stephen Roche called it quits in 1993 and was enthusiastically getting on with the rest of his life, racing cars and learning the public-relations business. Laurent Fignon, another star who left the sport in 1993, showed up at the start of Paris-Nice the next March, shaking hands, joking with friends and wearing the biggest smile he has displayed in years.

Sean Kelly seemed at least as happy as Fignon. But the Frenchman was walking around in jeans and a lumberjack shirt; the Irishman was in shorts and the jersey of the Catavana-Corbeil team, and he was standing on the Paris-Nice podium for a warm introduction to the few dozen fans out that early on a Sunday morning. Kelly was bubbling over now that he had managed not to retire.

It was a close thing, but he finally signed a contract early in March for his 18th season as a professional. His last one too, he insisted.

Didn't he say that last year? Was this once again his last season?

"Once again," he repeated, picking up the nuance. Then he corrected the record: "I said last year it was very possible it would be my last season, but I never said, 'Yes, it's my last season.' This one is certainly my last season. If it's a good one, a very good season — if I win a classic race, for example — it's still my last season."

He looked up, challenging anybody to contradict his version. For reasons not revealed, but obviously financial, he decided to continue for one more season — but did not make the decision until late in November. "Maybe I waited a bit too long," he added.

"At that time, a lot of teams were full, some of the bigger teams had a lot of riders and their budget was finished. And some of the bigger teams had a program that was very heavy. Some of them wanted me to do the Tour of Spain and the Tour de France, and that's something I didn't want. This team, the program suited me."

In its first year, Catavana was a low-budget French promotional team that had enrolled a handful of neo-pros and a handful of longtime pros who couldn't find a better-paying team. The veterans included Kelly, who would turn 38 in May. King Kelly, the winner of 33 races in 1984, the dominant classics rider of the mid-1980s and the man who topped the world professional rankings from 1984 through 1988.

King Kelly? He was an emperor. His classics record includes two victories in Milan-San Remo, two victories in Paris-Roubaix, two in Liège-Bastogne-Liège, and three in the Tour of Lombardy. A victory in the Vuelta a España, two victories in the Tour of Switzerland, and seven consecutive victories in Paris-Nice. Consider his record in 1986, when he won his third consecutive Super Prestige Pernod award as the season's top rider: first in the Grand Prix des Nations, Tour of Catalonia, Paris-Nice, Milan-San Remo and Paris-Roubaix; second in the Tour of Flanders, Paris-Brussels and Tour of Lombardy; third in the Vuelta and fifth in the world road championship.

With age comes decline. As he started the new season, Kelly ranked 86th in the computerized world rankings.

A criterium is not much of a bicycle race to win — just an exhibition, really — but it's all he won in 1993. He did it in the Netherlands in July, when almost every other star was competing in the Tour de France.

"This year wasn't a very good one for me," he agreed that fall. "I had a crash that knocked me out of the classics for a while, out of Liège-Bastogne-Liège and the Amstel Gold." Coming out of a left turn, he crashed in the Flèche Wallonne in mid-April, straining his groin. "If you get knocked out for two weeks, that sets you back an awful lot," he explained.

The transfer period for riders who are moving to new teams officially opened October 1, but anybody who waited until then was in grievous trouble. For a star like Kelly, a rider who commands — or at least asks for — a big salary, that fall could have been a worrisome time. Kelly denied that it was.

"I never really worried about it," he insisted at Paris-Nice as he sat in the team car and chatted. "I always thought it was possible to find the right team."

Catavana appeared to be that team, he said. One advantage was the lack of pressure: "It's a smaller team, a smaller-budget team, so the pressure will be less. On a bigger-budget team, there's more pressure because the money is being put in there and they want results." Catavana had a budget of not quite $1.5 million.

Could he still win a big race? "I think I'm capable of winning classics, yes," Kelly replied when he was still at large. His hard gaze, those cold eyes, could be felt over the phone. His fourth place in Paris-Tours in October, followed by an honorable Tour of Lombardy were proof that his strength was back.

"The motivation is there now," his agent, Frank Quinn, said from Dublin. "We got him a reasonable deal." Months before, Quinn was saying, "We're willing to take a fair reduction in salary from this year." A year when Kelly was believed to have earned about $600,000 from the Festina team based in Andorra.

That's a lot more money — about 100 times more — than Kelly earned when he began his professional career in 1977. "I've seen a lot of change," he agreed. "The bicycles have changed, the style of racing, the standards have improved, as they have in all fields of sports.

"There are many more riders now at a higher level than there were in the 1980s. Then, you had 15 or 20 riders at the top and there was a step down to the next. Now, you have 60 or 80 riders up there."

Are the riders better now or better trained? "When you train better, you become a better rider," he replied. "You have to push yourself to the limit — that's what makes the top riders. Some people can't do it, but that's what makes the good ones and the great ones."

Contributing to the change in the sport is the new freedom allowed riders to race for themselves and their own victories rather than work slavishly for a team leader.

"It definitely makes the racing more difficult," Kelly said. "Tactics have changed and it's much more difficult to plan now. When everybody worked for a leader, the leaders battled it out among themselves. Now you never know when the right break is going to go. It can go from the start or at any point in the race. Back then, it was always in the last 50 kilometers. So you could sit back and wait for those last 50 kilometers. Now you can't."

As he neared the end of his career, Kelly voiced no regrets. "Regrets," he said, repeating the word. "No, I wouldn't call it regrets. But if I could go back and start my career again, there would be things I would change, of course. Everybody would.

"The number of races — I rode too many. I was going from one race to another, at the beginning of the season especially." He estimated that for years he rode 160, "170 maximum," days a season, or 40 to 50 days more than are customary now. "Then, by the time the Tour de France came around, I paid for that."

Although he finished as high as fourth in the Tour in 1985 and fifth in 1984 and won the green points jersey a record four times, he was never a contender for final victory. He refused to use his heavy schedule as an excuse. "Let's say if I had an easier program up to the Tour, well then I would have had a better performance, that's sure. Winning is another affair."

His ambitions in his final season had little to do with the Tour. The classics were another matter.

"I hope to get into shape for the classics in the month of April," he said as riders continued to be introduced at Paris-Nice. "I'm starting a bit behind the other ones and it's going to be difficult the first two or three weeks to find the rhythm. After three weeks, I should be okay.

"In the winter, I did the normal preparation, as other years. I never let up in the winter. When I took the decision in the month of November that I was going to go on, I continued training right through the winter." By his first race, he estimated that he already had 5000 training kilometers in his legs, having gone out six times a week, from three and a half to four and a half hours each day, depending on the weather.

"I have a good foundation," he judged, "but I need a couple of weeks of the rhythm of racing."

Looking far down the year, he admitted that he was uncertain what came next. "No plans yet," he said. "I'll go back to Ireland and I'll have to do something, but just what I haven't made any decision yet." There was no rush, he implied, no rush at all to reach another November and another choice about the rest of his life.

By November, after a season without victory, Kelly decided that the time to retire had arrived. He won a final, ceremonial race back home and continued to ponder his future. Among other projects, it was rumored that he would tutor Graeme Obree in his transition from track to road. What a pair they would make: Kelly, who sometimes nodded his head to answer questions in a radio interview, and Obree, who was ready anytime, anywhere to talk about anything.

❋

GRAEME OBREE WAS JUST BEING FACTUAL WHEN HE EXPLAINED WHY Philippe Ermenault beat him in an exhibition in their first meeting since the 1993 world championship pursuit race a few months before. "He was hungrier for revenge than I was," Obree explained as his fingers plucked at the rainbow-striped champion's jersey he wore. "I've got this, you see, so I wasn't out for revenge."

As a put-down of the French rider who won the silver medal to Obree's gold, it would rank as a classic if Obree had meant it with any malice. He didn't. Life was very good those days for Obree and he was enjoying himself too much to feel any ill will.

It wasn't always that way. A little more than a year before, Obree decided that he was through with bicycle racing. "I was totally fed up with cycling because I had nothing from it whatsoever," he said.

He did not mean honors since Obree had won a fair number of amateur races in a dozen years of competition in his native Scotland. He meant money. At the age of 27, Obree, a dropout from studies in engineering and economics at Glasgow University, the bankrupt owner of a bicycle shop, was unemployed and broke.

"On the money side, I was on the dole and that was it," he continued. "I had no money and a mortgage and a wife and a son. Last October, I said, 'I'm through with the bike, I'm never going to ride again.' But there's not a lot of jobs floating around in Scotland, so soon I was thinking about making a comeback and what I was going to do was write a book about my experiences.

"Then a friend said, 'You don't have an ending.' What I needed was just one goal for one season for the ending of this book."

Obree paused and his face broke into a smile, possibly at his own bravado. The goal he chose was the most revered distance record in the sport: the world hour record. One man on a bicycle riding alone on a velodrome for 60 minutes.

Since Henri Desgrange, the founder of the Tour de France, set the first record of 35.325 kilometers (23.55 miles) in 1893, it had been pushed up by a line of champions. Fausto Coppi covered 45.848 kilometers in 1942, Jacques Anquetil reached 47.493 kilometers in 1956, Eddy Merckx reached 49.431 kilometers in 1972, and Francesco Moser broke the 50-kilometer barrier — as big a psychological wall as the four-minute mile — in 1984, when he covered 51.151 kilometers. Nobody had exceeded Moser since, although a few had tried and many, including Greg LeMond, had talked of trying.

"The hour record is everything," Obree said. "There's only so many people who have held it." They number less than two dozen, including Coppi, the five-time Giro d'Italia and two-time Tour de France winner; Anquetil and Merckx, each the winner of five Tours de France; Moser, the winner of the Giro and innumerable classics, including Paris-Roubaix three times — and Obree, the most feared time-trial rider in Ayr, Scotland.

Then, on July 16, 1993, on the bicycle track in Hamar, Norway, the Scotsman covered 50.689 kilometers in an hour, falling 462 meters short of Moser's record. "I said I'm going again tomorrow" … and spent a sleepless night after the decision, fearing leg cramps.

Riders usually space record attempts three or four days apart but Obree did not have that option since the officials who had to time his ride to make it official were leaving late the next morning. "What drove me on," he said, "was desperation. Desperation, necessity. It was the last chance."

Had the money for the record attempt run out? "Hardly," Obree said. "I didn't have any in the first place. Basically I didn't have any money and I saw my chance of getting any money slipping away. If I could humanly do this thing, I was going to do it."

For the second attempt, he changed bicycles, riding one he designed and built himself partly with material from the family washing machine. Designed without a top tube, the bicycle had a distinctive curve to the handlebars, which Obree grips with his 5-foot 11-inch, 160-pound body in a tight and nearly flat aerodynamic tuck, far over the bars. The position, usually described as "an egg," was his alone.

He set off early for the velodrome. As he remembered that day, it was 8:50 a.m. when he got to the track and he was nearly in a frenzy. "Where's my bike? Right. Where's my helmet? Right. Let's go. Then I got on the track and did a few laps" to warm up.

"Normally, the starter fusses about but I was wanting none of that. I said 'Okay, you ready?' and I just went away. And once you start, you're doing it, that's right, you're doing it."

And he did it.

Riding his revolutionary bicycle valued at about $100 and jutting far over the handlebars as he pushed a monstrously big 52x12 gear, Obree became the new holder of the world hour record. He had covered 51.596 kilometers … or 445 meters more than Moser. The gunshot that signaled his breaking of Moser's record came with more than a minute of the ride left.

Obree held the record barely a week or until Chris Boardman, then a big rival of Obree's in English amateur time trials, completed 52.270 kilometers at Bordeaux. But the Scotsman went on to win the world pursuit championship, a title he won on the same track in Norway where he set his hour record.

"So many people still think of me as the hour recordman, not the world champion," he mused. "Although I held the record only seven days, I'm one of the names on the list now. It was my one chance of doing anything, of winning anything, of being one of the big names."

He was anything but bitter, he insisted, that his hold on the record was so short. "I was expecting it," he said of Boardman's success. "Because it wasn't my best possible performance, because I'd ridden the day before. But it may be the best thing that's happened. Now I have another go at setting the record next year. Thanks to Mr. Boardman."

Obree was shown a photograph of him crossing the finish line at the end of his hour's ride with his right hand cocked into a fist in the air and a grimace mixing exhaustion and triumph on his face. What was he thinking then?

He looked silently at the photograph for what seemed to be a long time. Then he spoke: "I thought, at last, after all these years, at that moment....

"The best was when the gun went before I actually finished the whole hour. When that gun went, ah! Nothing could go wrong — I couldn't finish or a puncture or the fork snapped before I got to the end. If I dropped down dead then, if I dropped down dead, my epitaph would be written already. I had broken the record.

"After all those years of struggling and saving pennies to buy a loaf of bread, it had all been justified. Everything had been justified, all those years. Everything had been justified as soon as the gun went.

"As soon as the gun goes, that's me covered the distance he covered already. Everything else was extra. The gun goes after you've got the distance, it's a distance record. I was sailing and if I'd wound up dead, I'd still have the record."

Since then, and especially since he broke the world 4000-meter record in 4 minutes 20.894 seconds, while winning the world pursuit championship, Obree has had few financial worries. Professionally, the curve ran in the opposite direction: In what many regarded as an act of spite by the lords of the sport, his bicycle was banned at the 1994 world championships and he lost his jersey.

Turning professional, Obree rode that year without much success in a handful of road races and with great success on the track at the six-day races that fill the European fall and winter. Hard times were definitely over.

His schedule was full until the road season begins to replace the one on the track, said Martin Coll, 29, Obree's brother-in-law and briefly his manager. "We go to Grenoble tomorrow, two days later it's Dortmund, two days later it's Geneva, four days later it's Munich, three days later it's Bordeaux. We have to go from Bordeaux to Ghent to race there and then straight back to Bordeaux and we race two days there and then to Vienna, a week's invitation to Vienna.

"He'll be appearing for one or two days at every six-day event. He doesn't have to do the whole six days, just individual appearances. This is a money-making thing for Graeme."

Obree compared his new life to a merry-go-round. "You don't know who's the person who's going to pick you up at the airport, you don't know what hotel you're going to, you have no facts and figures."

Life had changed a lot. "Totally," Obree said. "In terms of security. You can't have a good outlook on life if you can't afford anything, so my outlook on life has improved. Otherwise I'm the same guy, except I don't see my wife as often."

He seemed a bit surprised to be asked why he was riding the merry-go-round.

"Why?" he echoed. "Because it's my job. It's what I'm good at. At the moment, this is what I'm good at and you know what they say: Do what you can when you can.

"I'm also doing it for the money. I've got to get as much money as I can. But it's got to be performance-driven. I'll do the performance, Martin will try to get as much money for me as he can. Obviously, we go to races where the best money is if there's not too much traveling involved.

"What money means to me is not all those zeroes in the bank, a fancy car or whatever else. It's no more sitting there and thinking what I can't afford to buy.

"You won't live any longer by having money; life will be just as short as it would be without money," Obree decided. "You've got to make the most of life."

That includes the book he planned to write a year before. "I'm still going to write it," he said, "but obviously it will be a bit different. Especially the ending. The ending will be nine-tenths of the book now."

7 Changing Sides

SOMEWHERE ON THE TOUR DUPONT'S LONG ROAD FROM
Wilmington, Delaware, to Winston-Salem, North Carolina, the public changed sides
… crossing over from Greg LeMond to Lance Armstrong.

The next era in American bicycle racing edged closer. It might have been too
early for anybody to cry "The king is dead, long live the king" — the Tour de France
in July would help determine how true that was — but by the end of the DuPont,
Armstrong ranked no lower than prince regent. That's the fellow who rules during the
absence or infirmity of the nominal sovereign.

How infirm LeMond was remained a question. But there was no question about
his absence during the Tour DuPont: 22nd place overall, laggard finishes in both
time trials and struggles in the mountains. At the end, he was 10 minutes 39 seconds
behind the winner, Viatcheslav Ekimov of the WordPerfect team. LeMond's only
consolation, he said, was "Maybe this is a good sign because I've always done well in the
Tour de France when I've done badly in the DuPont."

And vice-versa. He had not done well in the Tour de France, or any other race, since
1992, when he won the DuPont. People were beginning to notice even in the United States, where professional bicycle racing attracts scant attention.

When the 12-day DuPont began in Wilmington, LeMond monopolized fan
interest. At the short prologue to the race, Armstrong went barely noticed in his rainbow-striped jersey as he pedaled to the start, passing the GAN team car in which
LeMond awaited his turn. The car was surrounded by spectators, many of them car-

rying cameras and some of them carrying children. Everybody wanted a memory of LeMond. As he moved to the start line, the streets of Wilmington rang with cheers, which were renewed when LeMond finished fifth in the prologue.

"At the start, I didn't hear the cheers," he said. "I wasn't paying attention. I get nervous for these prologues, I'm concentrating. At the end, I might have heard a little bit. It's a blur — when you do a prologue it's a blur. When you go warm up on the course it seems like it takes forever. And then you go do it — and whoosh! A couple of kilometers later, I'm just getting into it — and whoosh!"

Armstrong, meanwhile, was 25th on a cold and rainy evening. "I rode like a grandma," he admitted ruefully, meaning he had been far too cautious about crashing on a stretch of wet cobblestones. "The weather didn't help me. I hated the weather."

But if the first part of the DuPont belonged to LeMond, the second part, when the real racing began, belonged to Armstrong. After all, he was the contender. They love a winner in the United States, or at least a contender. The public turned out in gratifying numbers at the sides of the DuPont's many roads through Delaware, Maryland, Virginia and North Carolina, and at its daily small-town starts and finishes. What these fans read about in their newspapers and saw on their television was no longer LeMond but Armstrong, and their allegiance shifted from one American to the other.

The script was perfect for people who turned out to cheer "U-S-A, U-S-A," as the pack went by: Armstrong, a Texan, working to overtake Ekimov, a Russian. This typecasting became even more pointed as Ekimov stayed on Armstrong's rear wheel and rode defensively, refusing to attack but following each attack by his rival. The public didn't know it, but that is the way stage races are ridden.

"To say it doesn't bother me, I'd be lying," Armstrong said, "but that's just the way the sport is." Tell that to newspapers and television more accustomed to reporting on stock car racing — the daily theme became Ekimov as a somehow unfair shadow of Armstrong's.

"The guy in second place," said Armstrong, referring to himself, "looks like the champion now, he looks like the fighter, he looks like the guy who deserves to win. And the guy in the leadership role, he looks like he's just sucking wheel.

"The only comfort I can take is that I know there will be a point in time when I'll be in that position. Because my time trialing is going to develop more and I'm going to have the ability to take time in the time trial. I can play that role. But certainly it's frustrating now."

Sitting in a condo in Beech Mountain, North Carolina, being measured for new racing shoes, Armstrong was in an expansive mood — even for him.

Perhaps it was his victory in that day's stage. "I needed to win a race," he said. "It's been too long since I won a race."

He was definitely happy and relaxed. "Racing in America is nice," he said. "Being in America is nice." He noted that this was his fourth Tour DuPont. "People like to say we have a big problem with fans coming to the races. But you come into some of these finishes with so many people there and you tell me we have a problem. The few races we have here, they're huge. We got the people out at the races and they sure make a lot of noise. At the start this morning, I couldn't get near the team car, I couldn't even walk around. I'm not used to that."

In the mornings, when fans are allowed to wander the staging area and ask the riders for autographs, it was indeed Armstrong's team car that they flocked to now. Although LeMond continued to attract the public too, it was obvious who won the loudest cheers at the daily sign-in and introduction.

Even if the fans thought he would win the DuPont, Armstrong knew better because of the final time trial. On past performances by each of them, Ekimov was a distinct favorite.

"I've got to look at the whole discipline of time trialing," Armstrong said. "That's something I've got to work on. The more I do, the more I'm going to be comfortable in that situation, the better I'm going to get." While that was a splendid long-range goal, he tried to remain upbeat about his chances the next day. He spoke without particular bravado and his words reflect a champion's spirit: "I can't look at it and say, 'I'm going to get my butt kicked, I'm going to lose 30 more seconds, I'm going to get second in the race.' I don't look at it like that.

"Maybe he has a terrible day. What is it now, 34 seconds, I wouldn't say that was impossible. What if he has a bad day? What if he has a flat? What if he has two flats? What if he misses the start? So many things can happen.

"And I'd rather get second than get third, so that's some motivation there."

In the end, he did get second, not third and definitely not first, because Ekimov easily won the time trial into Winston-Salem. Overall, Armstrong finished 1:24 behind. "All I can say is I did my best and it wasn't enough," he said at the final news conference. Asked when he felt he had no chance, he answered tartly, "At the finish line today. I thought I had a chance to come back, but Ekimov was superstrong. Anybody who wins both time trials like that deserves to win the race.

"I'm disappointed, I'm not overly happy. This is the second year I've finished second, so hopefully next year I can improve on that.

"I'm still young and inconsistent," he admitted. "I'm moving up in the ranks. I can get better."

LeMond? He could get better, too, and had to do it soon.

⊛

THE HOTEL ROOM MUST GO FOR $125 OR $150 A NIGHT, AND THE bicycle leaning against a wall would fetch $3000, maybe $4000. Bobby Julich — formerly one of Armstrong's teammates on the U.S. national amateur team — was sitting up in bed, eating a banana and watching something on a big color television set, waiting for his turn on the masseur's table downstairs. Goodbye to hard times ... that was last year.

Julich is bright, articulate and glaringly polite. He is patriotic, in love, and devoted to his parents. Mainly, at age 22, he was one of the great hopes of American bicycle racing, a tall, lean rider who climbs strongly, time trials well and holds his own in a sprint.

Most teams would have been happy to have a young rider with his attitude and talent under contract, people thought. They were wrong, though. Because an opportunity was missed, because his luck turned wrong and his timing went bad, Julich spent 1993 riding in the United States as an independent professional without a team, a sponsor or a support staff. He was alone in a team sport.

Food and water during a race? "I had nobody waiting in the feed zone," he remembers, "so I just carried everything. It looked as if I had a little backpack on.

"Many times I ran out of food, many times I ran out of water. Coming through a feed zone, once in a while I would try to snag a bottle from somebody but, more times than not, they would pull it back."

Massage, which riders receive daily during a stage race to refresh their leg muscles? "No such thing. I didn't have a rub for the whole year. I threw my legs up on a wall, if I had time and energy ... and just rub them down a bit, keep the circulation going, maybe use some baby oil."

Travel money and other expenses? Julich went through $25,000 in savings as he paid his way to and from races. "You start to throw away an empty water bottle during a race and then you think, 'They cost $5 each. This is going to cost me $5.' And if you have to throw away three bottles, you think, 'Five dollars each, this is costing me $15.'"

Race results? "I didn't have many major results," he continued in a flat voice.

"I was close but no cigar in quite a few instances. I forgot how to win, I forgot the winning attitude, I forgot the whole approach to winning."

That was 1993. In 1994, Julich was riding as a member of the Chevrolet-L.A. Sheriff team and had just finished the Tour DuPont in a splendid seventh place among the 112 riders who started.

He enjoyed the DuPont, Julich said at the finish in High Point, North Carolina, a bleak, furniture-making center where wing chairs outnumber people. He was pleased with his performance and with his team's, he said. He had enjoyed the racing, the life and the attention.

The attention, ah the attention — press conferences, interviews throughout the 12-day race, fans asking for autographs, the loudspeaker blaring his name and team at the start of each stage. The year before, he was anonymous.

"There are so many good riders out there, and you never hear of them because they're not on teams," he said. "I'd come to the start line in a race and I'd have on a jersey that was blank and they'd say my number but not my name; and two or three guys behind me they'd say, 'Oh, there's X with Coors Light or Y with Motorola or whatever.'

"You couldn't get on a team because no one knew you were in the race."

That wasn't it, of course. That was later. There was another reason earlier.

As a rider who finished fifth in the DuPont in 1991, when he was a 19-year-old member of the U.S. national amateur team, and then 10th the next year, Julich received offers to join professional teams. In retrospect, the best offer came from the Gatorade team in Italy at the end of the 1992 DuPont.

"The offer was there, but I was kind of talked out of it," Julich explained. "I was 20 years old and a bit intimidated by going all the way over to Europe and not knowing Italian, not knowing anyone on the team.

"And I was a little bit scared by the whole European regimen. I thought that people who just aren't ready and go over to Europe and get thrown into the meat grinder just get spit out. And that's not what I wanted.

"I really enjoy cycling in Europe, but if you're over there alone, you need to stay sane. And I don't know if I would have been able to stay sane not knowing the language, not knowing a soul, not having an American teammate."

He liked better an offer from Mike Neel, formerly the coach of the 7-Eleven and Spago teams, to join a new American squad funded by the Italian bicycle company, Rossin. "Mike has a reputation for bringing around young riders, for bringing them to success," Julich said of Neel. "He offered a team with half its races in

America, half its races in Europe. I thought that would be the best deal for me, to get my feet wet in my first year as a pro, half over in Europe; but if things went bad, I'd be able to come back to America."

The sponsorship for the new team fell through, as it sometimes does in the sport, and Julich found himself without an employer as the 1993 season was opening. The precise date, he noted, was January 26, "when I was waiting for my first pay check, for the go-ahead to have our training camp in Santa Rosa, California, the next week. Instead, on January 26, I was left high and dry.

"I frantically called every team in America — Saturn, Coors Light, Motorola, L.A. Sheriff, IME … everyone. Just looking. I told them I understand you guys have made your budgets already. Just get me to the races, you don't even have to pay me.

"That wasn't good enough because, as I found out on my own last year, just getting to the races is a major, major expense. Even if they didn't pay me, it was still going to cost them between $20,000 and $30,000 in lodging, transportation, equipment, all that sort of thing."

He did not call the Gatorade team in Italy. "I figured I had my opportunity there and I didn't take it and …" A long pause. "… I was kind of embarrassed to call and say 'I wasn't going to go on your team but my contract fell through and can I get back on?' I had enough sense not even to ask.

"So I raced as an independent all year. What drove me was to convince a team, regardless that it was late in the season, that Bobby Julich was a worthwhile rider to have on a team. Time and time again, when I would get results, I would go around to see if anybody was interested. Still it was no takers."

At last he received an offer to join a Portuguese team, for the few weeks that constitute the backbone of the American racing season. "It was a Portuguese quote professional unquote team that was more of a club team — just a bunch of guys over here for a free vacation. They promised to pay me, but they didn't pay a single thing. I was supposed to go over and do the Tour of Portugal with them and maybe stay in Europe the rest of the year, but that fell through. The ticket never came in the mail. But at least I got into races without paying an entry fee.

"What was a kind of bummer was that I'm from America and I'm very proud of that, and I had to wear a jersey that said Portugal on it. So everyone thought I was from Portugal. People would say, 'Gosh, you look like a guy that was on the U.S. national team last year' and I'd say, 'That's me….'" His voice was subdued now.

"And I finally cracked mentally and financially. In early August."

❋

DAYS LATER, WAITING IN THE MORNING SUN FOR THE AIRPORT SHUTTLE that would start him home to California from the Tour DuPont, Julich was relaxed.

There was nothing to worry about, he knew. What the organizers of the DuPont had not taken care of, his Chevrolet-L.A. Sheriff team had. His bicycle was bundled into its traveling bag, his luggage was at the curb, the shuttle to the Greensboro Airport ran dependably every half-hour, his plane ticket was confirmed.

People had seen to things. Life was easy for Julich in his comeback from a year as an independent professional. That year, nobody except Julich saw to things.

"I would go to the races, get there on my own, be really tired when I was starting a race because of all the logistical stuff — calling the organizer, making the plane reservation, making the car reservation. But that was the easy part.

"The hard part was getting on the plane, paying for your bike, once you get to your destination, get your bike, get your stuff, rent a car. By this time it's probably 9, 10 o'clock at night. Then you try to find something to eat, drive around when you have no idea where you are, look for some buffet thing, all you can eat, some low-priced thing, try to get a decent meal and stay away from the food poisoning that sometimes goes hand in hand with those all-you-can-eat places, and then after that try to get close to the race site and find a hotel.

"And by that time it's usually 12 or 1 o'clock in the morning and you have to get up and drive an hour to a race and it starts at 9 o'clock. You're up at 5 trying to eat. It was just a couple of hours' sleep a night.

"So it was difficult before I even started a race. And then, getting into the race, I had to cover every breakaway. If there was a Coors, a Saturn, an L.A. Sheriff and a Subaru, I had to be on it, no matter who it was, when it was, because that's the combination that's going to go up the road.

"And if it wouldn't work, I had to come back and another would go and I had to go again. I had to go with every single breakaway that looked dangerous to me, just to make the money to keep going."

And so, at last, he cracked.

"It was a series of cracks really," he explained. "More of a three strikes sort of thing.

"The first major crack came when I was unable to do the DuPont" in 1993 because major multiday races do not admit independent riders.

"That was when I realized I'm in big trouble. I always had a positive attitude and figured a team would pick me up by DuPont time. And when I was sitting on my couch in California and watching the prologue on TV, I really had a little problem there. I was depressed beyond all belief. I was pretty much ready to bag it right there."

He credited both his girlfriend Angela and John Eustice, a former rider and now a race organizer and television analyst, with helping him through. Eustice linked Julich with the Portuguese team that rode in such major U.S. races as the Thrift Drug Classic in Pittsburgh and the CoreStates uspro Championship in Philadelphia.

By the CoreStates, Julich continued, "I started to come on, I started to feel strong. I was in the final breakaway. After 155 miles, with five more to go, we got caught. That was the second blow. There I was in a seven-up breakaway and even if I got seventh, it was going to be about $5000, which would have done amazing things for my financial status and my morale.

"I believe if I had had that result, even seventh, some team would have picked me up. After that, I got depressed again for a couple of weeks and again my girlfriend pulled me out."

Several weeks later, at two races in California, he took the third strike.

"I went to a race in San Rafael and it was so hot, about 110 degrees — honestly. I started the race with what I thought were two water bottles, but I guess when I turned my bike upside down to get it in the car, one of my bottles fully drained out." With no support staff, Julich had nobody to pass him more water.

"I got dehydrated, cramped up, wound up making no money. The third strike was that I had never missed a race in my life, but the next day I missed the race in San Jose because I thought it was at 4 and it really was at 2:30.

"And that was a sign right there. I had never missed a race, I had never made that mistake. And that was it for me.

"I just went into major depression from there, which taught me a lot about myself. I never thought I'd fall into major depression — you hear a lot about it happening to people, but I never thought it would happen to me."

How bad was his depression? Bad, very bad, he answered.

"I didn't want to do anything, I didn't want to leave the house, all I did was sit there. The only time I went out was to get food. All I did was watch tv. I was a total slug.

"I spent so much of my time watching tv and thinking, 'When am I going to pull out of this?' And that day wasn't coming. That signal never came.

"I felt as if I hadn't raced in years. I'd read about the guys racing or watch them on TV and think, 'Gosh, I used to do that.' My girlfriend tried to pull me out of it, but I think I was pushing her away. All I wanted was to be left alone.

"Finally…." A tortured pause. "I remember sitting there and I felt so fat and I'm usually pretty skinny, and I looked at myself in a mirror and I was so embarrassed." From a weight of 160 pounds on his 6-foot frame, he had ballooned. "I had been a successful athlete … and in a month, a month and a half, my whole life had gone to pot. I felt like a total failure for the first time in my life."

Writing off 1993, Julich decided to try one more time to find a team for the next season. "I think many people could have bowed out and said, 'That's it.' But I've always had a competitive instinct and I couldn't say it," he explained. "I felt like I've never been a quitter. If I'd given up, I would have learned that when things get hard, just give up."

One thing he did learn, he continued, was that he was not alone: His girl-friend and his parents in Glenwood Springs, Colorado, helped bring him out of his depression. "Luckily, I have a really strong family that really cares about me and a girlfriend that really cares about me … and those were the people who pulled me out of my state.

"Sponsors, teammates, friends — people like that come and go. But only the people who love you are there no matter what."

Julich resumed training in California and began phoning and faxing teams to ask about a job for 1994. In November, the Chevrolet-L.A. Sheriff team made an offer.

"I said, 'I'll take it.' There was no counteroffer by me, no bargaining."

Dave Lettieri, the directeur sportif for the team, is pleased with his new rider. "He's a young guy, very talented," he said during the DuPont. "He fits in well and we're very happy with him."

Up to the DuPont, Julich had recorded seven victories. "Once I found a team, I began to feel like an athlete again," he said.

Still, Julich refuses to describe 1993 as a lost year. "In retrospect, last year was the best thing that could ever happen to me as a person and an athlete," he said. "I matured light years. I know now when things go bad, it's just for a brief time. You have to trim off the peaks and fill in the valleys because life and sports are an ever-lasting roller coaster.

"The lesson I learned last year was an overdue lesson. I always had it handy for me. I may have deserved a lot of things I received, but I wasn't appreciative; and now

I've seen the other side of the fence, I know what it's like, how hard it is, and I don't believe anyone can become successful without all the help you get."

Julich's story would come full circle by the end of 1994, when he signed for the Motorola squad, and became reunited with his former amateur teammate, Armstrong.

8 At the Start

JUST FINISHED WITH THE TOUR DE FRANCE'S PERFUNCTORY MEDICAL examination, Lance Armstrong was sitting at a table, reading a magazine, and in a sour mood. Definitely sour.

What had the doctors said? "They said I could start," he reported with an empty laugh. Had they said he could finish? "I'll say that. It depends on my legs and my body. It may not be in my best interest. Last year, it was the first 10 days … and then it was day to day. Maybe it'll be longer than that this year.

"I don't want to jeopardize the second half of my season just to finish the Tour de France," he continued, talking, posing for photographs and thumbing through the magazine at the same time. "I'll make that decision at one point or another." Officials of his Motorola team would obviously have something to say, too. "Partly, it'll be a team decision," he conceded.

Something was bothering Armstrong. Perhaps it was the hurry-up-and-wait atmosphere of the huge convention hall in Lille, where the 81st Tour de France was going through its paperwork and preliminary drills.

A year before, in his first Tour, Armstrong had been thrilled by everything about the race, including the medical examination. Let others scoff at the doctors' cursory check, barely more than a photo op — Armstrong was excited to be in what he termed "the show."

This time, he appeared to be blasé. Perhaps he was trying not to show that he felt any pressure about being the world champion in a race that he certainly was not going to win, and almost certainly not even going to finish. Considering his age and the fact that he would defend his world championship a month after the Tour, a withdrawal before the last, grueling week in the Alps seemed sound. And yet, he was the world champion and the man with that title might be expected to ride as long as he could and as hard as he could.

"It's not my first race as the world champion," Armstrong pointed out somewhat testily. "I had the first part of the season to get used to that responsibility."

He expected a hard race, he said. "I've only experienced one Tour de France and it was very, very difficult. I'm certain this year's is going to be as difficult, if not more.

"It seems to be much more difficult this year for some reason," he continued. "There's a lot of guys that go much faster this year. I'm just as fit and feel just as good as I did last year, but my strength within the peloton has sort of gone down. A lot of riders are stronger."

The obligatory question about his goals brought this: "The first one is the team time trial, because I think we can do super-well there. I'm motivated for the stages in England. They look fairly difficult. I have to look for my opportunities, because the first 10 days are the days I'm in the race and they're not necessarily the days that suit me. And it's not easy to win a stage when the course doesn't suit you. But many stages do suit me — the ones in England and possibly the one that finishes in Boulogne.

"But you can't win a stage in the Tour every year. I mean, you can if you're winning the Tour, if you're Indurain or Rominger. That's another level."

His most recent race, the Tour of Switzerland, left Armstrong with mixed feelings about his outlook for the Tour de France. "It was good for a while, but harder than I expected," he admitted of the mountainous Swiss race. "I was making hard efforts there to be competitive and be a factor in the race, but those 2000-meter climbs — I'm just not cut out for that. But I was happy with it, and if I could have the form here that I had there, it would be helpful.

"Still, I'm hopeful and I feel much better than I did last year — even if I do have this," he said, moving his leg from under the table to reveal a large swelling that spread over his right knee. So that was what was bothering him.

"I got it in Holland, my whole leg was infected," he explained. "It's a bite. All the way down to here," gesturing low on his shin, "the whole leg was swollen. The swelling is going down, but it was nasty for a while." He said that he had taken antibiotics for a few days and that they had affected his condition. "For a few days in training, I couldn't even get out of my own way. I think it's receding now. Two days ago, my whole calf was swollen."

A couple of days later, relaxing at the Motorola team hotel in a village outside Lille, Armstrong reported that his leg was no longer a problem. His mood was now upbeat. Definitely upbeat. Even if he did start with a complaint.

"What a great hotel it is!" he said sarcastically, gesturing at the typical chain hotel. "I read that the Tour de France is the most profitable sporting event in the world ... and we're staying in this dump. Somebody's getting rich. For finishing in Nowhere, France, okay. But you can't tell me there's not nice hotels in Lille — it's a big city." In fact, there didn't seem to be any nice hotels in Lille, he was told. All in all, there was a lot to be said for staying in the cool and calm boondocks rather than steamy and noisy Lille.

But Armstrong was enjoying his complaint too much to pay attention. Pulling up a lawn chair near the hotel's swimming pool and opening a bottle of soda, he lacked only a barbecue to be a perfect suburbanite. To a visitor, the surroundings and the country air seemed much more pleasant than the greasy smell of french fries that hung over downtown Lille.

"Millions and millions of people are going to spectate this thing," he ranted on. "It's the biggest bike race far and away, and they're just underachievers when it comes to hotels." Smiling contentedly, Armstrong paused for breath. He was definitely enjoying himself. "Yeah, I'm upbeat," he admitted. "I was downbeat with the leg a few days ago, because I didn't know. The problem was I had to take some antibiotics and they made me feel terrible, which they'll do."

The start of the Tour made a convenient reference point to look back at the season and ask Armstrong how he thought he was doing.

"It's average," he said. "A lot like last year — up until this point, it's been pretty close." Except that he had not repeated his million-dollar victories in the United States. "Europeans don't look on that as a result," he countered. "It was just a media frenzy. So I was second in the DuPont and won a stage, just like last year. I was better in Liège this year. At this point last year, I had won five races, three of them in that Triple Crown thing. Now I've won three, but didn't win one in the early season the way I did last year.

"It's harder to race this year, cycling is harder now. In a year, I tell you, man. I hate to point fingers, and I'm not going to do that, but there are a lot of guys who are a lot better and a lot faster than last year.

"The rainbow jersey — it's so much harder to race with that. Even if you're bad in that jersey, they're going to follow your every move. Say if some guy won the championship on a fluke — took off on the gun and got 30 minutes and held them off — and was an undeserving world champion, everybody knew he was terrible, the next year when he was in the jersey they would still follow him around. Every move. Because of that jersey. It just sticks out, it sticks out to the eye. People assume it's dangerous."

But he was indeed dangerous.

"That's what I'm saying: When you combine somebody who can be dangerous with that jersey, then they *really* follow you around.

"I think I can do better in the Tour. If I can show some improvement in the time trials and the climbs and we can do well in the team time trial, that's successful for me. Those big climbs in the long, high mountains, I can't compete yet. When you're dealing with the Indurains and the Romingers when they want to go, then you're really in trouble." But he was hopeful about becoming a better climber. "A few years ago, if we rode a 2-percent grade, I was off the back. When I was an amateur, I was a terrible climber. But I improved in that and lost weight and now I can climb fairly well. So I may be continuing to rise. It's coming naturally.

"I don't know how this leg is going to affect me, I don't know how the antibiotics hurt me, I don't know how I'm going to recover. So I just may have to start slow and then pick it up, whereas last year I was always very aggressive in the beginning. Every stage, I was sprinting. I was sprinting for like 10th place, I was always aggressive.

"This year, I'm going to have to control that and be selective. Unless it's incredibly hard and I can use my strength to get away, they're not going to let me get away. Nobody will."

❁

LIKE ARMSTRONG, GÉRARD RUÉ WAS SPENDING ANOTHER BICYCLE season far from his native country. He frowned. First Switzerland, now Spain. "It seems like a nice country," said the Frenchman, "but of course I don't know much about Spain yet. It's only been a month or so."

He was more decisive about Switzerland, where he spent a year as a rider for the Helvetia team. "It wasn't easy to get along with the Germans," he said, declining to elaborate. When he left Helvetia after the 1991 season, Rué complained that a French rider — this French rider, in any case — found it difficult in a country where the food, language and customs were not French.

Everything was French with the Castorama team, which Rué rejoined. Castorama, sponsored then by Système U, was his team from his professional debut in 1987 until he went to Switzerland in 1991. Rué had productive years with the French team, but none as good as that season with Helvetia: sixth place in Milan-San Remo, second place in the Critérium International, third place in the French championship, 21st place in the world championship, and a splendid 10th place in the Tour de France.

Still, it was Switzerland.

Rué is very French, he conceded. He was born in Brittany and likes everything about France and being French. Not quite everything. He frowned again, his eyebrows arching, his long chin jutting.

He had just been asked about the bicycle race that forced him once more into exile. That was the 1992 French national championship, a race in which Rué saw a chance to become as French as a professional racer can be: the national champion, the wearer of a jersey slashed with the blue, white and red of the French flag.

"The French jersey is a beautiful one to wear," he said. "Quite a distinction." His voice grew deep and lively. "I think that for any professional racer, the jersey of a national champion is most important." The thought made him sit straighter in his chair. Then he rubbed his thumb against his first two fingers. "That, too," he said.

Money, glory, the tricolor jersey, a career in France — Rué came within 8 kilometers of them all in the French championship. Half a lap before the finish line, he was off alone, 35 seconds ahead of the pack and feeling strong, when his teammate Luc Leblanc led a charge to overtake him. Setting the pace for a handful of rivals, Leblanc soared by his astonished teammate. So did those who traveled in Leblanc's slipstream. Rué finally finished seventh, 40 seconds behind Leblanc, the winner.

A rule of the sport is that teammates do not attack each other; if a rider is alone at the front of the field, a teammate blocks for him, trying to slow rivals, not speed them along. "If Leblanc hadn't attacked, Rué would have won," said Laurent Fignon of the rival Gatorade team. "You don't do that when you have a man ahead. It's a little disgusting." That was quite a condemnation coming from Fignon, who attacked a teammate and towed along a handful of opponents in the 1989 world championship, allowing Greg LeMond to win.

Leblanc was unapologetic. "I'm sure Gérard understands," he said after climbing down from the victory podium and embracing his mother. "We were both strong ... but that's the way races go. Too bad there's just one jersey."

Stomping away from the finish, Rué was furious. "With a lead of 35 seconds and half a lap to go, I would have won. Amazing, a teammate is the one who catches me. You understand me, I've always been straight with my teammates. I'm proud that I've always been straight with them.

"I deserved better. I don't know what anybody else thinks of his victory, but for me, it's Luc's victory, not the team's."

Later, Leblanc was asked if he thought he and Rué could continue to work together on the Castorama team. Oh sure, he answered. "I know what he'll be going through in the next few hours. You think I've never been disappointed in a race myself? I'm disappointed for him. But only the jersey counts and I've wanted this jersey so much for so long. I would have gone to the ends of the earth to win it."

Raymond Poulidor, the French bicycling favorite a quarter of a century ago, has long known Leblanc and is fond of him. Nevertheless, Poulidor sums him up this way: "Luc's a kid. A nice kid, but a kid." He spoke after the French championship, but before the 1992 world championships in Spain, where Leblanc again defied team strategy by attacking alone near the finish, pulling rivals with him, while the French were attempting to keep the leaders together and set up a sprint finish for their best sprinter, Laurent Jalabert.

Rué was on that team, too. By then, he had announced that he could not stay with Castorama another season.

Still bitter? Rué was asked the next spring, in Fontenay-sous-Bois, a Paris suburb, where he was awaiting the start of the Paris-Nice race.

"*Oui, mais oui,*" he replied. "It's a bad memory, the worst I have."

But there was a bright side, he continued. Now in Spain he rides for Banesto, the No. 1-ranked team in the sport, led by Miguel Indurain.

"It's a new atmosphere with Banesto, and I like it," Rué said. "I like it in Spain, because the sport is so strong there now. There are only three big teams in France and it's not a good thing for French cycling that half the French riders are with foreign teams.

"Banesto ... we're a little like a family. With Castorama, it was good times too, but....

"I had four years with Castorama, and they were good years. And then the last year wasn't so good. After the championship, I had to get out." He would not say more about Leblanc or the race, preferring to talk about the present and future.

With Banesto, Rué's obligations were clear: "In the Giro and Tour de France, I'll ride for Indurain; but in the classics, I'll be on my own. I hope to do something there. And then, of course, there is the French championship again." A final frown.

Now it was time for Rué to go. "*Au revoir*," he said. Then, with a smile, he acknowledged the response: "*Adios*."

9 Those Were the Days

THE PHOTOGRAPH SHOWED A YOUNG GREG LEMOND, AN ALMOST incredibly young Greg LeMond, even for those who had known him a dozen years. Thin, blond and boyish, he wore a blue sweat suit as he stood on a platform and had his hand shaken by an adult. On both sides of them stood other youths, all obviously members of a team.

"You remember?" asked an old man, speaking French. He was standing in a hotel restaurant outside Lille (a much better hotel, incidentally, than the one Lance Armstrong was staying in and complaining about), and had come up to the table in the bar where LeMond sat with a couple of reporters after dinner.

"Sure I remember," LeMond answered, and he really did. "That was after a stage I won in the Circuit des Ardennes in 1980."

"That's right," the old man said. "Me, I'm the one shaking your hand."

"I couldn't forget that day," LeMond told him. "I won the stage and that night I stole the team car and went to the velodrome where the stage finished and drove at 90 kilometers an hour. I still remember that."

Looking a bit startled, the old man invited the rider to join him and his friends at a nearby table. LeMond parried the request politely — "Maybe a little later, I've got to talk now with them" — and the old man left happy.

"We didn't steal the car exactly," LeMond continued, in English now. "We snuck out of the hotel and took the team car. I wanted to drive in Europe so bad, so we took the team car and went to the velodrome, opened the gates and drove around at 50 miles an hour. Jeff Bradley and me." He chuckled. "It really felt good. We were laughing so hard. I remember it so well." Always easy to like, LeMond becomes at moments like these utterly touching.

LeMond at 19: Did he think then he would win three Tours de France?

"My dream was to win it once, if I could," he replied. "When you're a kid 18 years old, 17, all you dream is to win the Tour de France.

"There are a lot of 17-year-olds out there doing it, but I tell you it's a lot more difficult than people think. If I knew how hard it was, my dreams at 17 would have been changed.

"What they say when you're young: You're capable of everything. As you get older, you're a little more skeptical, more cautious." He was still smiling as he peeked now and again at the photograph.

He might be a little more skeptical in principle, but not in practice, LeMond continued. "I know I can race well. But it takes time to get myself back. I feel things are coming on." His condition, he went on, was "good but just not super. I've had the DuPont, the Dauphine and the Tour of Switzerland as stage races — that's not enought to be world-class level. Everybody else is non-injured, nobody else is having health problems, they're having good seasons, they had good winter training — it does make a big difference.

"It's been frustrating: I've really worked hard since last October. I'm trying to keep my morale up, I'm trying to keep my motivation. If I can get through this Tour intact and in health, if I can get a little rest afterward, I could have a very good August. I see no reason why not. In stage racing you reach a plateau —" his hands began moving high and low "— and the ups and downs become less, and all of a sudden you're in good condition and you're up there with everybody."

The bar area of the hotel lobby was becoming noisier now that dinner was over and LeMond, though tired, was willing to talk a while longer. Pleasant and friendly as always, he signed autographs when fans approached his table and even posed twice with women for photographs taken by their husbands. He attracted a lot of attention for somebody who was "just GAN's road captain," he was jokingly told.

"Road captain?" he asked. "That's what they want to say, but what does 'road captain' mean?"

Then try the term "super *équipier*," which Roger Legeay, GAN's directeur sportif, was using to describe LeMond in this Tour.

That one hurt.

"Road captain is one thing, but super *équipier* is another," he said, bridling. "I don't like that term because it means I'm not here for my own ambitions. I have my own ambitions: I want to try to win a stage. An *équipier* can kill himself. After two weeks he's dead. For me, the important thing is to try to finish the race in health, not too tired.

"Super *équipier* — that's Roger's way of trying to take the pressure off me from everybody saying, 'Why aren't you in the G.C.?'" or overall standings. "There's been a lot of talk that I'm going to be a worker on this team. I'm not going to be any more of a worker than anybody else on this team.

"If conditions present themselves like they do now [his teammate Chris Boardman won the prologue], I'm going to work for him to help Chris keep the jersey. It's good for us.

"But I'm not just going to blow all my chances. I don't want to give up hope before I start the race. I'm here to race for the team, but I feel if I do well and am aggressive, that's good for the team. It's not just me going for a stage win, it's me being at the front so that other GAN riders can possibly win a stage. To me, that's a good teammate. The guy who just goes up and rides at the front, that doesn't mean anything to me and I'm not going to do that."

Whatever role was being staked out for LeMond, he knew very well that it was no longer team leader.

"No, no, no. I think I start equal with everybody else," said the man who had won the Tour de France three times.

❊

ALL OF LeMOND'S VICTORIES — AND THOSE OF MANY OTHERS — have been witnessed by the event's current director, Jean-Marie Leblanc. Unusually, in the Tour's nine-decade history, Leblanc is the first former professional racer to become the race's director of competition. He was named to that post late in 1988 after nearly two decades as a journalist, mainly as the chief bicycling correspondent of the French daily sports newspaper *L'Équipe* and as editor of the monthly magazine *Vélo*. Leblanc talked about the changes he has seen in cycling in the following interview.

Question: You raced from 1966 to 1971 and participated in two Tours de

France, in 1968 and 1970. How good a rider were you?

Answer: I was a minor professional, nothing more.

Question: And you became a journalist while you were still a rider?

Answer: Yes, but I didn't do both jobs at the same time. I became a journalist, covering boxing and cyclo-cross, during the off-season. In 1971, I decided that my real future was in journalism.

Question: Is it true that as a rider you earned 500 francs (then $90) a month?

Answer: True. It was the minimum wage.

Question: And now some riders make close to $2 million a year. How do you feel about today's salaries?

Answer: Good for them. What bothers me is that some riders make big money before they have results to justify it. It's one thing to win big money in a race, another to earn a huge salary and not win races. That's what drives up the cost of sponsoring a team. In my day, riders made their money through salary, prizes and criterium contracts. Now riders seem to care only about their salaries. We offered $50,000 to the winner of the final time trial in the World Cup one year and hardly anybody bothered to show up.

Question: Shortly after you were appointed to the Tour job, you said "We must create races for the year 2000." What does that mean exactly?

Answer: We mustn't necessarily maintain, in 2000, the same races as in 1930 and 1950. Bicycling evolves, as does its environment, social and economic conditions and the concept of leisure. So bicycling must keep its great classics while looking for new paths. An example is the Bordeaux-Paris race. When I was young, Bordeaux-Paris was the monument of suffering — more than 600 kilometers overnight and all the next day. Today we wonder, "Why doesn't Bordeaux-Paris work any more?" There are, of course, economic reasons: the riders don't want to do it any longer. But really one of the main reasons is that riding 600 kilometers on a bicycle doesn't impress anyone any longer. It isn't heroic. Everybody does Bordeaux-Paris. Cyclo-tourists do it every year, television journalists did it a few years ago to raise money on a telethon. Bordeaux-Paris became banal. There are so many other things in sports that are superior in suffering and effort.

Question: What other races have become outdated?

Answer: Traditional six-day races on the track. Before World War II, people said, "Riders go six days without sleeping, that's amazing." Today, a six-day race lasts a few hours each evening. They don't impress anybody.

Question: And what has replaced Bordeaux-Paris and six-day races in esteem?

Answer: Triathlon, for example, among the young. Or mountain biking. We must deal with this or else we will look like an archaic sport. I'm always irritated when I go to a city welcoming the Tour and it sponsors a show of bicycles from 1900. Put in a bike from the year 2000! Make the young dream!

Question: Despite your attention to the future, you're very much a man of tradition, aren't you? Aren't you the one who restored the traditional finish of Paris-Roubaix at the velodrome in Roubaix rather than in front of the factory that helped sponsor the race?

Answer: It was the first decision I had to make.

Question: Are you happy about it?

Answer: Yes.

Question: Because of tradition?

Answer: Yes. It's not a contradiction, though. I'm for modernization, but when we can maintain something that contributed to the sport's glory, like the finish of Paris-Roubaix at the velodrome, it must be done. At the factory, the finish was nothing. Now it's fantastic.

Question: What's your biggest fear for the Tour de France?

Answer: I'm afraid of how gigantic we've become. We're not elastic and we can't keep adding cars — always more cars for sponsors, for workers, for journalists. We can't do it, and I say, "Stop." The riders must have priority in the Tour de France. If we forget them because we keep adding sponsors and journalists, we remove the heart from the Tour de France. That's why everything else growing bigger around the riders scares me. Again I say, "Stop."

Question: Is it only the riders who will be hurt?

Answer: No, it's also a matter of where we can go. If we grow too immense, we will have to choose only big cities for stages. And then we will lose so much territory for the race that we will also lose our capacity for exploits.

Question: The days when a stage could finish in a village are gone already, aren't they?

Answer: They're not over, but it's difficult to fit a village in. We have three conditions: At the finish, a long straight road at least 450 meters long, 150 meters before the line, 300 meters after it; a hall, or at least a tent, that can be used as a press room, and lodgings for 3500 people within 30 or 40 kilometers of the finish. So, you see, some small towns are doomed.

Question: You've said that excess is the enemy of well-being. Can you give an example of excess that you're eliminating?

Answer: We used to have five or six finishes at altitude. That's excessive. I believe in a modern sport: No suffering for suffering's sake. The Tour de France must be a race that anyone can win, not just the best climbers.

Question: But LeMond and Indurain have won it?

Answer: They're not just climbers. They're all-arounders.

Question: In the last decade, the Tour has started in Switzerland, Luxembourg, Germany and Spain. Will it ever be possible to start in the United States?

Answer: No. When I took the job in 1989, Montreal was bidding for the start in 1992 and we had to make a quick decision. There was a lot of enthusiasm over there. I organized a poll among the readers of *Vélo* magazine, real fans of the sport. I had 200 of them called on the phone and asked, "Do you like the idea of starting the Tour in Montréal?" The answer was 50-50. And I thought, can we displease 50 percent of our fans? Then there were considerable logistical problems. Finally, there was the risk. Not of a plane falling in the Atlantic, it's not that. But the risk, say, of leaving behind a rider in Canada, or of a rider or two getting sick there because of the long flight and change in food and water. Or coming back to Europe and having a rider do badly and complain "It's because of jet lag." We risked a bad atmosphere at the start, and a bad atmosphere can ruin the entire race. So we'll go to another place if it's close — Spain, Switzerland, Holland — but Tokyo, Montreal, New York, no. You can't take risks with the Tour de France. You've got to be modern but not exaggeratedly modern. There's a limit.

Question: Do you think professional road racing has a future in America?

Answer: I don't know too much about it, but I was struck at the 1990 Tour de Trump by the size of the crowds and by how many young people were watching the race. I was also struck by the finish in Boston — a Sunday and the roads were blocked to cars. All those empty roads! That meant that the authorities understood that bicycling is important. However, there are drawbacks too: the United States is so huge that it's hard to stage races from one city to another. Then there's the outlook once Greg LeMond retires. Will Americans still care about professional racing? That's what I don't know. What counts for Americans? The Olympic champion, the world road race champion, the Tour de France winner. And that's it.

Question: Seventh or eighth place in the Tour de France doesn't do it?

Answer: No. In Europe, we appreciate that kind of result, but in America they like only stars.

Question: What's the future of women's bicycling?

Answer: It's a problem in Europe. Women's bicycling is a young sport and I think that the Tour de France Féminin happened too quickly. It gave the illusion that women's races were already at the top level. In the first Tour Féminin in 1984 there were 60-odd riders and the difference in quality between the top riders and the lowest was enormous. The race was a good idea promotionally, but as a sports event it was premature.

Question: After 1989, when Greg LeMond made up 50 seconds to win the Tour on its last day, why hasn't there been another time trial at the finish?

Answer: That time trial was scheduled before I took over and I didn't think it was a very good idea. I thought that once the Alps were over, the Tour would be decided. We were really lucky that year. If the yellow jersey can't be caught in a final time trial, it's pointless. And it deprives the pack of a final day of glory on the Champs-Elysées.

Question: Do you have major changes in mind for the Tour de France?

Answer: Nothing spectacular. There are things that need changing, though, like the problem of jerseys. I think the public doesn't understand all the jerseys, the confusion. You remember in the '70s, jerseys were easily recognizable: orange was Bic, red was Flandria, black and white checkerboard was Peugeot. Now they change all the time and the spectator can barely figure it out. The pack goes by — *phfft* — and the spectator recognizes nobody. That's something to work on.

Question: Are you hinting at a return to national teams?

Answer: That's possible. In 1982, at the start in Basel, I read the famous editorial in *L'Équipe* in which Jacques Goddet [then the race director] called for a return to national teams every four years. I read that editorial and thought, "He's right: Every four years a super Tour de France, an exceptional Tour de France. The World Cup of soccer is staged every four years, the Olympics every four years, why not a Tour de France with national teams every four years?"

Question: But the Tour had national teams from 1930 to 1962 and again in 1967 and '68. Wouldn't this be a step backward?

Answer: Twenty, 30 years ago, it wasn't the same. There were no Soviet riders, no German riders, no Colombians, no Americans. Now they're all here in force and it's possible to field 20 truly national teams.

Question: Do you think sponsors would accept it?

Answer: It will take a while to convince them. I've got nothing against a national team's jersey carrying the name of a trade team, as long as it's small. If a rider does well, his sponsor will get publicity. I'm certain the idea of national teams would be a success with the public. All we need is the intelligence to work it out and the courage to do it.

Question: The riders would cooperate for three weeks when sometimes they can't do it for one day in the world championships? You really believe that rivals like, say, Gianni Bugno and Claudio Chiappucci would work for each other on an Italian team?

Answer: Why not two Italian teams? Two Spanish teams? Both countries are rich enough in riders and trade teams to have two national teams.

Question: Where will the Tour de France be 50 years from now? Will there be a Tour de France in another half a century?

Answer: I'm hopeful. Bicycling, especially the Tour de France, has the advantage of a social, a cultural meaning. We have the French landscape as our background — harmonious, beautiful. The framework of our sport is magnificent: It's hot, it rains, it's sunny. We have the mountains and the sea. We're not locked into a stadium like tennis or soccer. What's difficult is respecting the traditions of bicycling and being modern at the same time. For every person who says, "You've ignored tradition, where are the Pyrénées?" there's somebody who says, "You're an old-fashioned sport, you've been overtaken by tennis and golf." That's the challenge that interests me. We have to preserve our balance.

[PART 2]

THE 81ST TOUR DE FRANCE

[PROLOGUE]

Apprehension
. . . and Excitement

AS THE 81ST TOUR DE FRANCE NEARED ITS START IN THE
northern French city of Lille, Greg LeMond's teammate Chris Boardman acknowledged that he had a chance to become a national hero, the toast of his native England. "I can see the opportunity," he said, "it's definitely there. This would be a
very, very big thing at home."

Nevertheless, he insisted, he was not excited. What was there to get excited about?
"Apprehensive, I believe, is the word," he said thoughtfully. "Excited, no."

Perhaps he would be excited if, as was highly possible, he won the prologue time
trial. "Perhaps then I'll be excited," he conceded. Cool wasn't half the word.

This was the humdrum scenario outlined for Boardman by officials of his
GAN team: He wins the prologue, stays atop the standings through the first three
stages in France, and then arrives in England for two stages there as the leader of

COR VOS

Chris Boardman's strong prologue in the 1994 Tour de France put him in the yellow jersey, only the second Englishman to do so — 32 years after Tom Simpson.

Fellow Englishman, Sean Yates (right), soon followed Boardman's performance by wearing the yellow for a stage in west France.

H.A. ROTH

Less than two years after
Greg LeMond's nearly fatal
gunshot wound, he was
back in the yellow at the
1989 Tour (bottom)
and a surprised but happy
winner at the world's (right).
His career would fade
on a less spectacular note,
as he ended his 1994 Tour
(far right) losing out to a rare
muscular disease.

Motorola avenged Armstrong's 1994 Tour DuPont loss to Viatcheslav Ekimov by dominating the 1995 edition from the start. Armstrong went on to win the overall title by beating Ekimov by two minutes.

Arnstrong's first season as a pro was capped with a solo win at the world's — not unlike LeMond's world's win 10 years earlier.

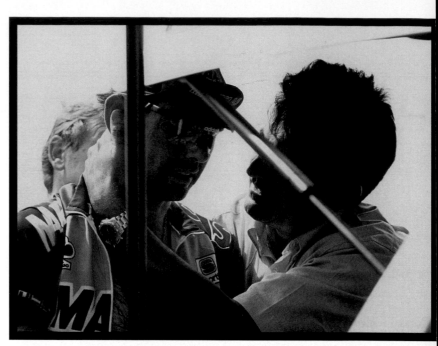

The 1995 Tour was
marked by both
Miguel Indurain's
(right) unprecedented
fifth consecutive vic-
tory and by the tragic
death of Motorola's
Fabio Casartelli in
stage 15. The follow-
ing stage started with
a quiet moment
(below right) and was
dedicated to the fall-
en 1992 Olympic
champion.

Though Rominger's
résumé includes the
world hour record and
wins at the Giro and
the Tour of Spain, the
Tour de France was
often the source of
frustration for the
Swiss star. Illness
forced him to aban-
don early in 1994
(above left), and his
eighth-place finish in
1995 was less than he
had hoped.

Armstrong dedicated his stage 18 victory in the 1995 Tour to his teammate Fabio Casartelli, who died after a fatal crash three days earlier.

the Tour de France, the man in the yellow jersey.

The yellow jersey! He could become the first Englishman to wear it in 32 years and the first to wear it at home since the Tour began in 1903. Who's talking excitement?

"Everyone wants to see the dream of bringing the yellow jersey to England now," Boardman admitted. "Now," he repeated. "But I'm not necessarily here to win the yellow jersey. I'm here for the experience." Try not to get excited.

Boardman, a 25-year-old native of Hoylake, near Liverpool, learned how to be cool, or how to pretend to be cool, when he won the gold medal in pursuit racing at the 1992 Olympic Games in Barcelona. "Crash media training," he called the furor over one of the few Britons to star in any sport at the international level. His training was intensified in July 1993, when he broke the world hour record on the track at Bordeaux, France, on the day the Tour arrived in the same city. His feat dominated the next day's editions of *L'Équipe* the daily French sports newspaper.

A few months later, Boardman was signed to a professional contract by France's GAN team, hitherto led by LeMond. By Tour time, the new leader — ruffles and flourishes for a neo-pro — was Boardman.

"He's a star now," said GAN's assistant directeur sportif Serge Beucherie. "He's comfortable in the mountains, he's comfortable in the pack, he's found his place. He had experience only on the track, he started from zero on the road and now he's at—" Beucherie paused. "He's at where he is now," he concluded.

Even Boardman was uncertain where that would be, once he got past the 7.2-kilometer (4.5-mile) prologue through the downtown streets of Lille, the Tour's unexpectedly lively host city. As befits a pursuit rider, the Briton's specialty was time trials, and he won both in the Tour of Switzerland, his most recent stage race before the Tour. He also got over the mountains well there *and* in his previous race, the Dauphiné Libéré. "He's much more at ease in a race now," Beucherie noted. For the early months of his first pro season, Boardman had to be surrounded by GAN teammates in a race, because he felt insecure in the tightly bunched pack after years of riding alone on the track and in English amateur time trials.

"I've been a professional for just seven months," he pointed out. "I mean that about being at this Tour de France for the experience. There will be other

Tours for me, I assume. But I'm under no illusions this isn't the most difficult thing I've ever done."

The pressure, he continued, was lower at the start of the Tour than it was when he was trying to break Graeme Obree's world hour record. "I could take second place in the prologue and be satisfied," Boardman said. "In the hour, there is no second place. So the only pressure I'm feeling is from myself."

Although he had been ailing somewhat for the last eight weeks with a chest infection, he said it had not hampered his performance. "I'm going very well," he reported. "My red-cell count has dropped," reducing the supply of oxygen to his muscles, "but I'm at 95 percent of my peak. Still, that does mean I'm lacking the 5 percent."

Perhaps the 5 percent was the excitement quotient. To the end of the interview, Boardman insisted he was calm. The closest he would come to denying it was when he said, "Sport is 90-percent disappointment … and it's the other 10 percent that makes it all worthwhile."

And added, "It's the ultimate dream, carrying the yellow jersey to England…."

The next day, he astonished the field by easily, oh so easily, winning the prologue, finishing 15 seconds ahead of Miguel Indurain in second place. The margin seemed immense over 7.2 kilometers and over the defending champion in the last three Tours. Indurain, of the Banesto team, won the prologue in 1992 and 1993.

Riding in hot and heavy weather through central Lille before a crowd of several hundred thousand, Boardman averaged 55.152 kilometers an hour, a tick better than 34 miles an hour. He caught the man who left a minute ahead of him, the humiliated Frenchman Luc Leblanc (Festina), who glanced back over his shoulder in amazement when the roar of the crowd and Boardman's long shadow both told him that he was being overtaken.

Third in the 189-man pack was Switzerland's Tony Rominger of the Mapei-CLAS team, 19 seconds behind Boardman. Rominger and Indurain were the two favorites in the 81st Tour de France, which would cover 3978 kilometers (2485 miles) before it finished in Paris on July 24. Boardman might not be there and certainly he would not make it to Paris as the man in the yellow jersey. But for now he was wearing that jersey.

Boardman was calm after his victory, dodging speculation about whether he could keep his lead during the next three stages in France and carry the yellow jersey aboard a train through the Eurotunnel and then home to England. Instead he talked tactics.

"I probably could have gone a bit faster in the first few kilometers, but I preferred to keep to a steady speed and not take the risk of blowing up," he said. He gave due credit to his bicycle, a modified version of the revolutionary Lotus carbon-fiber machine that he rode to victory in the Olympics. But not too much credit: Boardman resents suggestions that his bicycle, not its rider, is the secret of his speed.

LeMond also rode a Lotus. but the American was hampered by a loose seat that probably cost him 10 seconds and 10 places. He ended up in 22nd, four places behind Armstrong — who was 39 seconds slower than Boardman.

[STAGE 1]

The Battle of Armenteers

SIX UNEVENTFUL HOURS IN THE TOUR DE FRANCE'S FIRST STAGE ended in chaos in the last 20 seconds when a policeman standing on the course caused a crash that left four riders sprawled and bloody on the ground in Armentières. Three were hospitalized and two were so badly injured that they were out of the race.

The policeman was also hospitalized but not seriously injured. Tour officials reported that the policeman was taking a photograph as the leading sprinters tore for the finish line, 150 meters away. He was just far enough away from the barricade that holds back the crowd to be directly in the path of Belgian sprinter Wilfried Nelissen, of the Novémail team. Moving at a speed of about 70 kilometers an hour, Nelissen plowed into the gendarme, and they both fell.

Right behind the Belgian, and tumbling over him, were Frenchman Laurent Jalabert, of ONCE; Italian Fabiano Fontanelli, of ZG-Bottecchia, and Ukrainian Alexander Gontchenkov, of Lampre.

Jalabert was the most badly injured. For many minutes after the crash, he sat on the road with his face covered in blood from what doctors said were broken teeth and fractured cheekbones. Nelissen had a concussion and face and knee injuries. He and Jalabert, two of the leading sprinters in the sport, would not start the second stage. Fontanelli, who had face injuries, was expected to be released from the hospital in time to continue the Tour.

Riding just to Nelissen's left in the sprint was Djamolidin Abdujaparov, the Uzbek sprinter whose go-for-it style has caused crashes before. This time, though, the "Tashkent Terror" was blameless and, better, the winner of the stage. The Polti rider was timed in five hours, 46 minutes, 16 seconds for the 234-kilometer slog from Euralille, a district in Lille, to Armentières, a small city in northern France.

Second among the survivors of the sprint was German Olaf Ludwig, a sprinter with Telekom, and third was Johan Museeuw, a native of nearby Belgium with the GB-MG-Bianchi team. Finishing 29th and given the same time as Abdu' was Boardman, who retained the overall lead by 15 seconds over Indurain. LeMond and Armstrong also finished in the pack, respectively 69th and 86th on the stage.

This was the second consecutive year in which the first stage ended in a crash. In 1993, Abdujaparov was the villain in the sprint but nobody was badly hurt. In 1991, he crashed solo on the final stage in Paris, hitting the steel barricades that line the Champs-Elysées as he sprinted toward the line.

On the narrow roads that the Tour usually uses, crashes are not uncommon. There was an early and uneventful pileup in the first stage, for example, affecting about a dozen riders. All of them got quickly back on their bicycles, and continued to pedal through a monotonous landscape of two-story brick houses with red tile roofs, uncountable cafés advertising beer, an occasional field of wheat or corn, and massive numbers of spectators out to welcome the start of the Tour.

Crashes are most frequent in the early going, when the riders are still nervous and frisky, before the heat and the wear and tear of three weeks of racing leave them more willing to grant right of way to a rival. But this is rarely true in the sprint for the finish line, an exercise bursting with machismo, where to yield is to lose face.

To have one of the many policemen who line the course involved, however, was most rare. It was an ugly end to a stage that Boardman's GAN teammates kept easily under control. They were assisted by the heat (low 80s), an intermittent head wind, the length of the stage and the near certainty that the flat terrain would lead to a sprint finish.

The only attack of the day started with just 64 kilometers left and got nowhere other than the outskirts of Armentières, which is celebrated mainly as the home, in the World War I song, of the "Mademoiselle from Armenteers" — hinky, dinky, parley-voo? If anybody still felt like singing….

[STAGE 2]

Driving Hard for the Line

FABIANO FONTANELLI IS ONE TOUGH GUY, BUT THEN EVERYBODY knows that. He is, after all, just a lesser light among the Tour de France sprinters … and they revel in their reputation as tough guys. Nothing scares them, they say, or they would be *former* sprinters.

How tough exactly was Fontanelli? Enough so that, a day after the crash near the finish line put three sprinters out of the race and left Fontanelli bruised and aching on the ground, he was back to contest, yes, another sprint. Among the major crash victims, Jalabert underwent a three-and-a-half-hour operation for broken teeth and facial bones; Nelissen remained in a hospital under observation; and Gontchenkov was treated for a broken right arm. He had not realized that his arm was broken and shook off the pain to walk across the finish line and make his time official. The race's other sprinters would understand.

Twenty-four hours later, Fontanelli finished ninth, as the sprinters demonstrated that they could not turn cautious. A dozen drove hard for the finish line of the second stage, as usual swerving ever so slightly to disrupt rivals, and as always bumping shoulders and throwing elbows to clear room, racing head-down and hell-bent. There was even a ritual protest, disallowed, of interference.

On the line, the winner was Dutchman Jean-Paul Van Poppel, of the Festina team, who was first by tenths of an inch over Ludwig — the German who'd also finished second the day before.

Third after the 203.5-kilometer second stage from Roubaix to Boulogne-sur-Mer, a port on the English Channel, was Silvio Martinello, an Italian sprinter with Mercatone Uno. One-hundred-fifty-five of the remaining 186 riders were given the same time, five hours, 5 minutes, 40 seconds, which left the hierarchy unchanged. A day before the team time trial that was expected to shake up the standings, Boardman remained first overall by 15 seconds, but he and his teammates would have to ride spectacularly in the next day's race against the clock to bear the yellow jersey to England.

Boardman's biggest challenge was likely to come from Museeuw, whose GB-MG-Bianchi team won the previous year's team time trial handily and had the engines to do it again. Museeuw ranked seventh overall, 23 seconds behind.

Tucked down there on the list, in 23rd place, 39 seconds behind Boardman, was Armstrong, who had hoped to win the second stage — *if* the pack broke up on the final hill a few miles from the finish and had not been able to get back together for a sprint. Although the pack did split, it regrouped and Van Poppel became a rarity: He won a sprint while wearing the polka-dot jersey as the (temporary) king of the mountains.

Climbers are almost never sprinters, but Van Poppel is no climber. He won the jersey on the first bumps in the otherwise flat road of the first stage and lost it on a few more small hills during the second stage.

Armstrong, no sprinter, finished 25th in the stage into Boulogne. He hoped for far better. "Not just that it's the Fourth of July and it would be nice to win it," said the famous patriot before the stage. "The truth is I'm feeling motivated. Confident. I wasn't feeling confident until after the prologue." His problem was the insect bite that left his leg swollen, and curtailed his Tour training. Now the infection was gone, he was back in form after a splendid 18th place in the prologue, ("I could have done even better, but I didn't ride with confidence because of the leg"), and he was highly optimistic about the team time trial on a 66.5-kilometer course from Calais to the Eurotunnel … and the trains that would carry the Tour to England.

"The course is hard," he said. "Hilly, windy, windy. It's a circle course, so you have winds from every direction. I think we can win the team time trial. We were third last year, and now we have a better team."

[STAGE 3]
It's a *Team* Time Trial

THE DREAM ENDED FOR CHRIS BOARDMAN IN CALAIS — HE WOULD not wear the yellow jersey when the Tour traveled hours later to his native England.

He rode heroically at the front of his GAN team, powering it along for kilometer after kilometer on the windswept and hilly team time trial course. In the end, though, his teammates were simply not up to his pace.

"I'm disappointed, but that's racing," the even-tempered Boardman said afterward. "We did our best." GAN finished eighth among the 21 teams in one hour, 21 minutes, 48 seconds.

Far faster was GB-MG-Bianchi, which finished first in the long circuit from Calais to the nearby Eurotunnel under the English Channel. GB-MG was clocked in 1:20:31. That made Museeuw — a name that would not trip lightly from British tongues — the man in yellow when the riders boarded their special train and became the first large group of passengers to use the Chunnel, as it is known, since it opened two months earlier.

A 28-year-old Belgian and a top rider in classics, but not a man of the mountains, Museeuw now led the Tour by 10 seconds over Indurain, who was looking better every day. The Spaniard picked up 34 seconds on his major rival, Rominger, whose Mapei-CLAS team came in fifth, while Indurain's Banesto team finished a surprising third, 18 seconds behind GB-MG. Sandwiched between them was Motorola, which came in only six seconds down. That fine second place vaulted Armstrong into fifth place overall, 22 seconds behind Museeuw.

The team time trial was made especially difficult by winds off the English Channel, which kept flags snapping in the harbor of Calais, a major crossing point by ferry to England, 42 kilometers away. Although the chalk cliffs of Dover can be seen on a clear day, they were hidden in haze during the race.

Otherwise, the weather was ideally sunny and cool for the vast number of fans again out to see the Tour. For the riders, the stiff winds, which blew from all directions during the stage, were a problem.

Since the time of a team's fifth man across the line was given to all of the first five, the point was to keep as many as possible — but certainly five — of the nine starters together. That was not easy. Only the Telekom team from Germany had nine riders together at the finish and it did no better than 14th place.

Boardman's team had varied troubles keeping its five riders together, because of equipment failure, flats, near-crashes and fatigue.

"We set too hard a pace on the hills," said GAN's LeMond. Because of chain problems, LeMond fell slightly behind on the last hill, a Z-shaped road visible from afar because of the spectators thick along its sides, and the team had to wait briefly for him.

Then, a few kilometers later, Eddy Seigneur, another GAN rider, took a right turn badly and needed to take his right foot off the pedal to steady himself, before he crashed into a crowd barrier. Again, the team slowed to let him catch up.

At the front, Boardman was taking extraordinarily long turns. He may have been too strong and too eager for his teammates in this race. More than once, for example, he looked back to see if another rider was ready to replace him and serve a minute or two as the pacesetter. And more than once, nobody was up to the job … so Boardman had to keep leading.

The Englishman was losing his yellow jersey and he knew it, and there was nothing more he could do to help himself. As the name says, it's a *team* time trial.

[STAGE 4]

An English Summer's Day

LIKE THE WIFE OF BATH, THE PARDONER AND THE MAN OF LAW, the Tour de France set off to Canterbury ... plus Royal Tunbridge Wells ... and the Garden of England in southern Kent ... also Piltdown, hometown of the hoax prehistoric man.

The fourth stage was the Tour's first visit to England in 20 years and only the second in the bicycle race's history. Organizers' predictions that a million people would watch were "spot on" — as they say there.

So, on this day so full of Britannic resonance, who won the 204-kilometer stage from Dover to Brighton?

"A Spaniard?" asked a spectator, his voice rising in disbelief. "A Spaniard?"

Correct. Welcome to the new Europe. Francisco Cabello, a 25-year-old rider for the Kelme team with one previous victory in his five-year career as a professional racer, was the Spaniard in the works. He deserved his easy victory, too. Cabello broke away from the 184 other riders at kilometer 23 of the rolling and twisty stage, and saw only one rival again until he looked back at the finish line and realized that the nearest rider was 20 seconds behind.

It might have been even worse for the unbelieving spectator since the rider who joined Cabello at kilometer 55, rode most of the remaining 149 kilometers with him and then finished second, was Emmanuel Magnien of the Castorama team.

"A Frenchie?" would have been the incredulous cry had Magnien won. "A Frenchie?"

Cabello was timed in five hours, 12 minutes, 53 seconds for his ride on an overcast and cool afternoon that later turned into a drizzle — a perfect English summer's day. Finishing with Magnien, 20 seconds behind and in third place, was Flavio Vanzella, a 30-year-old Italian rider for the GB-MG team. Because of that team's victory in the time trial the previous day, Vanzella had ranked fourth overall, 22 seconds behind Museeuw. So when the Belgian finished with the pack, 18 seconds behind Vanzella — who also gained eight bonus seconds for third place — the Italian now led Museeuw by four seconds, and so took over the yellow jersey.

Boardman did his best to justify the encouragement of the enormous crowds along the route. "Go for it, Chris" and "Good luck, Boardman" were favorite signs among the fans, many of them children in their school ties and blazers.

He did go for it, storming away from the pack just as it reached Brighton and riding strongly enough to finish fourth to major applause. He now ranked 17th overall.

The stage started at the 11th-century Dover Castle, complete with moat, drawbridge, slits for archers, and opportunities for a tourist to have a photograph taken with a soldier in scarlet tunic. The stage ended on a circuit that included a street called Old Steine in Brighton, hard by the garish and enchanting Royal Pavilion ordered to be built by George IV in the early 1800s.

In short, Olde England.

The Tour's two-day visit had been five years in the planning to avoid an embarrassing repetition of the 1974 stage in England, which was scheduled to publicize French artichokes. The riders were ferried on a chartered flight across the Channel to a military airport and onto an unopened highway, where they raced under the eyes of an estimated 25,000 enthusiasts — nobody, by Tour standards.

This time, the organizers got it right, closing roads, selling the fans beforehand on the Tour's attractions, filling the skies with television's helicopters and radio-relay planes. Air traffic into and out of Heathrow Airport was even rerouted and delayed to give the Tour airspace.

The blitz worked and the crowds were even vaster than they had been so far in France. If only Boardman or the other Englishman in the race, Sean Yates of Armstrong's Motorola team, had won.

"A Spaniard?" the man cried.

[STAGE 5]

They Loved LeMond

THEY LOVED GREG LEMOND IN BRITAIN, CELEBRATING HIM AS THE
first native English-speaker to win the Tour de France; and he won louder cheers from
fans at the riders' introductions before the fifth stage than anybody else in the pack.
His victory in 1986 remained green, as green as the rolling fields around Portsmouth.

But the two Tour stages in southern England had shown just how long ago
1986 was. Even LeMond's Tour victories in 1989 and 1990 seemed ancient as he continued to struggle to regain winning form.

Or simply form ... any sort of competitive form.

He lost more than five minutes when he faded on the final hill of the fourth stage,
into Brighton. This next day, he lost 2:46 more and found himself in 145th place overall, 8:53 down on Vanzella.

While nobody imagined he had a chance to win the race, the question was
how could he could make it over the first mountains, nearly a week away, since he
could not make it over small hills now. The 187-kilometer fifth stage, a circuit
from and back into the naval port of Portsmouth, should have offered few difficulties for him. It did not for most of the 181 other remaining riders.

In a sprint finish, the winner was Nicola Minali, a young Italian with the
Gewiss-Ballan team. Second, for the third time in the Tour, was Ludwig and third
was Martinello. Minali was timed in 4 hours 10 minutes 49 seconds, a speedy 44.7
kilometers an hour, on a cool and overcast day. With all the leaders matching the winner's time, Vanzella remained in the yellow jersey. His teammate Rolf Sørensen of
Denmark lost some time with a flat tire near the stage end, allowing Armstrong
to move into fourth overall.

Once again, English fans showed up in vast numbers in the villages, small
cities and narrow country lanes that the riders traversed. The race was an enormous success in England, even if its many team, official and journalist cars did per-
sist in driving on the right during the stage. Wherever the Tour is, it is always

France — a truism that inspired one of the few criticisms during the two-day visit. The high Tory *Daily Telegraph* bemoaned that "The Tour ... is, true to Gallic tradition, self-obsessed, self-important, self-promoting."

It is also the world's greatest bicycle race and the tens of thousands of fans who cheered LeMond during the introductions remembered that. He might not have won a race since 1992 but he remained a champion in England. LeMond looked drawn and weary during the applause and more so at the finish. Seeking help, he met before the stage with his former coach, Paul Köchli, a Swiss who ran the La Vie Claire team in 1986, when LeMond first won the Tour. Köchli, who now was a consultant to both riders and Swiss journalists, is considered to be an expert on training and conditioning. Although he did not reveal what he and LeMond discussed, it was obvious.

"My condition now?" LeMond said a few days before. "It's good, but it's just not super. My condition is good," he repeated. "It's just on the uphill there's a little doubt.

"I'm trying to keep my morale up, I'm trying to keep my motivation. If I can just get through this Tour intact and in health, if I can get a little rest afterward, I could have a very good August with World Cup races and the world championship."

Unbelievably, the three-time winner of the Tour seemed to be saying that he regarded it as no more than a preparation race this time.

Not really, he explained. "I still want to try to win a stage and have a good Tour. I don't want to give up hope. I've been known to make tremendous improvement in a race."

He thought briefly about that possibility. "It's unlikely I'll make *tremendous* improvement," he continued, "but it's possible. I mean, I've worked hard, and sooner or later it's got to come around.

"It's so simple to say it's my age, it's so easy to say that." He turned 33 late in June. "It's the simplest excuse, but I'm a complicated case.

"I've been bothered by gunshot wounds, tendon surgery — the hunting accident in '87, I was two years away from cycling. Last year, was a total catastrophic year for me.

"I go through each week saying it's over for me, it's over for me, it's too hard," he confessed. "And then all of a sudden I feel a little better and I change my mind."

The final question was whether he was riding this Tour de France as his farewell. "I don't need to say farewell to the sport," he said firmly. "I want to do the Tour for myself. I have perfect explanations why I haven't been doing well and, regardless of all my problems, I still have a desire to win again. And that's what keeps me going."

[STAGE 6]

The End of the Road

GREG LEMOND REACHED THE END OF THE ROAD IN THE TOUR DE France and in his glorious career, too, dropping out of the race, exhausted, on a small hill, the Côte des Loges-Marchis, during the sixth stage. Let the records show that the finish came at kilometer 183 of the 270.5-kilometer ride from Cherbourg to Rennes.

Radio Tour, which connects all cars in the race, reported that he had dropped behind to help relay an injured teammate, Didier Rous, back to the pack. That sounded good, but was not true, LeMond said later; he had dropped behind because he was exhausted. Part of the way up the hill, LeMond simply could not continue racing.

His abandonment was the biggest of many shocks during the stage.

Another was a change in the wearer of the yellow jersey. The new man in the jersey was Sean Yates, 34, the Motorola team's powerful English rider. Yates finished sixth in the stage, two seconds behind the winner, Gianluca Bortolami, a talented Italian rider with Mapei-CLAS. Bortolami was part of a seven-man breakaway and sped away from his companions with little more than a kilometer left.

Second was Abdujaparov and third was Swiss rider Beat Zberg, of Carrera-Tassoni. The main pack, including the previous man in yellow, Flavio Vanzella, finished 46 seconds behind after a disorganized chase of the breakaway group.

Bortolami, who now trailed Yates by just one second for the leadership, was timed in six hours, 58 minutes, 47 seconds. That made for a slow stage in cool and windy weather before a fair turnout of fans, as the Tour de France returned to the mother country after two days in England.

"You can't choose where you'll win the yellow jersey," joked Yates, who rode close by his home in southern England two days earlier and, granted permission by the pack to take off alone, stopped to greet his parents at the side of the road. Overshadowed in this Tour by the other Englishman in the pack, Boardman, Yates took some revenge as he celebrated. "I'm just as big a name in England as Boardman," he said with satisfaction.

The stage was jokingly referred to as the Tour's "Longest Day" — both because of its length and the fact that it celebrated D-Day 50 years before. On the trip from Cherbourg in Normandy to Rennes in Brittany, the race wheeled past Utah Beach, where U.S. troops landed, and through Ste. Mère-Église, the first town they liberated from the German invaders.

Then the riders competed in a special D-Day Sprint in the city of St. Lô, from which Allied troops broke out to begin their advance eastward in 1944. The winner of the sprint was Ludwig — the German sprinter. (Whatever irony the French felt, they kept hidden.)

LeMond was still in the pack at that point and lasted two hours longer. Only that morning, after the two disastrous stages in England in which he lost more than eight minutes, he said that he continued to suffer from chronic and unexplained fatigue. Perhaps, he suggested, the answer was lead poisoning from the dozens of buckshot pellets remaining in his body since he was shot. Perhaps, he also suggested, he had worked too hard in the team time trial and had not recuperated as thoroughly and quickly as he did in his glory years. Despondent, he had offered many variations on "perhaps" in the last few days.

For the first time, LeMond left the Tour in its broom wagon, denied the face-saving ride to the finish in a team car. He took a seat on the left, halfway back in the small bus, and slumped in despair. However he went, he went out a champion.

LEMOND WAS LYING ON A MASSEUR'S TABLE AS OTTO JÁCOME WORKED on the muscles in his back. The curtains were drawn and just one light was on, making the room even gloomier than it had to be. Open suitcases sat on the floor, partly filled with clothes and bicycle gear. Neither LeMond nor Jácome spoke until the rider began answering questions, speaking not in his usual articulate flow but in bursts and bits. Like his speech, he was shattered.

"I haven't been able to recuperate in a race this year," he admitted. "I was accelerating, but it was one of those hills, one hill too many. I was killing myself to stay with the group and I didn't have any juice left. I just ran out of juice."

LeMond corrected the Radio Tour report that he had dropped back to help his injured teammate. No, he said, he dropped back because he could not stay with the pack himself. LeMond would not lie to put himself in a better light, to hint that he had become exhausted while helping a teammate. The truth, he continued, was that he had been thinking about quitting all during the stage.

"It went through my mind all day. But I kept thinking, 'Maybe I'll feel better, maybe I'll feel better, maybe I'll feel better.' It gets to the point where you know you won't feel better but you keep hoping.

"It's been since the team time trial. Even the day before that. I'm just fried. I have to struggle so hard."

Jácome had moved his hands now from LeMond's back to his legs and the rider turned on his side and allowed the first look at his face. His eyes were red and obviously he had been crying.

"It's not that fast," he said of the race. "I've been in Tours much harder, much faster. And that really opens your eyes. After five days, six days of the Tour.... I spent two years...." He searched for more words, wanting, needing, to explain.

"Regardless of what a lot of people think, I have desire to race. I had high motivation all winter, but I just keep getting knocked down. Right down to the ground.

"If I can't be competitive, I don't want to continue. If I'm healthy.... That's what I want to prove to a lot of people.... I'm 33 years old, there's no reason I...." The phone began ringing in that small hotel room. LeMond was on his feet now, standing there, staring at the phone, hoping the ringing would stop. He was not going to answer.

"If I quit today, I'm happy," he continued when the room was quiet again. "I don't have to prove anything to anybody. But I'm a racer. It's not to prove anything to anybody — it's to prove something to me.

"I do have desire," he said almost tearfully. "I'm somebody who loves to compete. An athlete loves to compete, but he likes to compete at the front. At least me. I don't want to be a domestique, I don't want to race races just to race races. And I feel that's all I've done for the last two years. I'm starting 'em just to start them.

"I'd like to perform. That's all."

He returned to the massage table, asking Jácome to work again on his back.

"Maybe this is just a little passage," he went on, brightening. LeMond's mood was shifting quickly now. "It's hard to know," he said.

"I'm realistic," he decided. "It's hard to keep motivating yourself. That's always been my strong point, persistent determination. But it gets to a point where you can't.... I want to go back....

"I've done a lot of tests for chronic fatigue syndrome and they show I have chronic fatigue. Why do I get it? That is the question: Why? I don't know."

His mechanic, Julien DeVriese, entered the room with a bicycle frame for LeMond to take back to his home in Belgium. He and his wife would gather the three children — the two boys were on a trip in the Alps — and leave for their home in Minnesota in a few days. DeVriese looked weary and sad and so did Jácome — they had been with LeMond for years and genuinely loved him.

"Life goes on," LeMond said with a sigh. "It does. Believe me, in one week I'll be enjoying myself in Minneapolis." He giggled. "I say that, but it's hard," he confessed.

"I shouldn't have come to the Tour. I was doubtful before and if Roger had said, 'Go home,' I'd have gone home. But we both said I'd try to do the first two weeks as well as I can. Not in my wildest dreams did I think I'd be out in six days."

His voice was very quiet now, the words sometimes lost in the sound of Jácome zipping bicycle bags in the background. "I thought I'd be out after two, three days in the mountains. Anyway." Zippers were being pulled, locks closed, suitcases moved. Exit, LeMond.

[STAGE 7]

Changing Fortunes

UP FRONT, WAY AHEAD, EROS POLI SAILED ON — ALONE AND DREAMING of victory. Out back, far behind, Didier Rous rode alone too, trying manfully to remain part of the Tour de France.

Neither rider fulfilled his goal. The seventh stage proved once again that the Tour is a great leveler of men and their ambitions.

When the pack finished the 259.5-kilometer stage from Rennes to the technology theme park of Futuroscope in western France, Poli, an Italian *domestique* for Mercatone Uno, was nowhere in sight. Exhausted by a long breakaway, he was caught and passed by the peloton, and finished the stage nearly 15 minutes behind the winner.

By then, Rous — a French teammate of LeMond's who was badly injured in a crash in England three days earlier — was a passenger in the broom wagon. Just as LeMond had been the previous day. Rous was not alone either, as three others abandoned. That reduced the field of 189 riders who started the race to 177.

A dozen of those remaining competed in the sprint finish that seemed predictable at the end of the flat stage. The winner was Slovakian Jan Svorada, who rides with the Italian team, Lampre-Panaria. Abdujaparov was second and Ludwig was third — giving the German three second places and a third so far, but no brass ring.

Svorada was timed in a rapid five hours, 56 minutes, 50 seconds, the same as most of the pack, on a stage that was conducted on a perfect summer's day, sunny and just breezy enough to be comfortable in the mid-80s.

The yellow jersey changed backs again as Museeuw reclaimed it from Yates by winning one time-bonus sprint and finishing second in another. Those bonuses put Museeuw ahead of Yates by six seconds.

The swift pace, 43.6 kilometers an hour, was mainly Poli's doing. He bolted away at kilometer 60 and opened a huge gap. Since he was so far down in the over-all standings — more than 10 minutes — nobody deigned to chase him at first.

Normally, he is a lead-out rider for his team's sprinters but had no job this Tour since one of them (Cipollini) was injured and the other (Baffi) had already quit the race. Why not, then, go on a solo adventure?

On Poli went — past hundreds of thousands of spectators, over the silted Loire River, past vineyards and fields of wheat, through alleys of plane trees — build-ing a lead that reached a maximum of 18 minutes 30 seconds. That was at kilo-meter 115, when the huge Poli, 6 foot 4 and 190 pounds, a gold-medal winner for Italy in the team time trial at the 1984 Olympic Games in Los Angeles, was still being ignored by the pack.

Then the peloton came to life, towed by teams with strong sprinters. As the speed increased, Poli, far ahead, and Rous, far behind, both suffered. Rous suf-fered more. Twenty kilometers before Poli attacked, the Frenchman slid out the back of the pack and first saw it leave him straggling.

Rous, a 23-year-old support rider who had been trailing since he injured his left leg in the crash, remained in the Tour on courage and the help of his friends. His GAN teammates had been dropping back to set a pace for him and allow him to ride in their slipstream and save energy.

But as soon as he regained his place in the main body of riders, he began falling behind again. The stage before, he had yo-yoed 15 times, finishing six seconds out-side the official time limit for disqualification. The judges were lenient, howev-er, and allowed him to continue.

Why did he hang on? Rous offered no public explanation.

Not a climber, the second-year professional could offer his GAN team no help in the mountains to come. Nor could he expect to do well in the coming individual time trial. The answer seemed to be that Rous continued because he felt unable to stop.

But at last he had to. At kilometer 141, a teammate, Francis Moreau, was told by GAN officials to save his strength and stop pacing Rous. Moreau rode up to the pack and, 13 kilometers later, Rous coasted to the side of the road and ended his ordeal.

At the same time, Poli was still building his lead. Passing the first of a half-dozen chateaus along the route, he remained more than eight minutes ahead of two chasers, Laurent Desbiens of the Castorama team and Mario Chiesa of Carrera. The pack was seven more minutes behind those two.

It was moving fast, however, and with 50 kilometers left, Desbiens and Chiesa were caught. Seventeen kilometers later, it was Poli's turn.

Turning and seeing the other riders approaching, he stopped pedaling, waved at a television camera and slipped into the stream of riders rushing to the finish. His solitary adventure had lasted 166 kilometers and four hours.

❄

SEAN YATES DESERVED BETTER. HE HAD NEVER WORN THE YELLOW jersey before in his 13 years as a professional, and his career had included so few personal triumphs that he deserved a longer stay in the jersey than one stage. But he wasn't complaining; Yates is a team worker ... an engine in team time trials ... he chases after opponents in other stages ... he's the finest descender in the pack ... a mentor to young riders — many things. But not a complainer.

"I've always liked helping others," he said a few seasons back, describing his role. "That's my motivation: leading out a sprint, working as hard as I can in a team time trial, keeping the others out of the wind. My job is a team man. What motivates me is riding for other guys."

Selfless? Yes ... and sincerely so. Eldest children are often like that. Perhaps he learned to look out for others while he was growing up in Sussex and helping to care for his four younger siblings. He also found time to win enough junior races, mainly time trials, to gain a berth as a pursuit rider on the British team at the 1980 Olympic Games in Moscow.

The year after that he turned professional with Peugeot, one of the pioneers in the "Foreign Legion" — Britons, Australians, Irishmen, Americans, Canadians — that began to transform what had been almost exclusively a continental European sport. But many of his fellow Anglophones reaped the headlines, not Yates. On that Peugeot team, Irishman Stephen Roche began winning races and Australian Phil Anderson wore the yellow jersey, while Yates merely rode support. In 1984, he helped Robert Millar, a Scot, win the polka-dot jersey of the Tour's King of the Mountains and record a fine fourth place overall. Yates was far down the standings.

In his five years with Peugeot, Yates won 12 events in England — a relative backwater of pro cycling — but only two on the Continent. And both of those were time trials. However, European victories started to come his way, after he joined Roche on the Fagor team in 1987. First came a win in the Grand Prix of Cannes, then, later in the year, a stage of the Nissan Classic in Ireland. Other wins followed in 1988: a stage of Paris-Nice, another in the Midi Libre, and a third in the Vuelta a España. Yates's high point was a 14-second victory in that year's Tour de France individual time trial, over 52 flat and windswept kilometers from Liévin to Wasquehal in northern France.

The next year, he joined the 7-Eleven team (which later became Motorola) and continued to pick up a victory here and there. But he was beginning to understand that he would never become more than a support rider. "I realized I was never going to be a superstar, so I concentrated on helping the team," he says.

Although Yates was planning to retire after the 1992 season, he changed his mind when Armstrong signed on with Motorola. Here, finally, was a promising superstar rider Yates could help mold. "His future is unlimited," Yates said of his teammate during the 1993 Tour. "I consider it my privilege to help him develop that future."

That works both ways.

Yates was indeed the lead-out man for Armstrong's Tour stage victory into Verdun, and he was almost embarrassingly a human sacrifice for Armstrong's victory in the '94 Thrift Drug Classic in Pittsburgh, slowing and waiting for the American to overtake him and cross the line first.

Yet the Briton has managed also to win a few big races himself. In 1992, it was the British professional road championship and in '94, the CoreStates USPRO Championship in Philadelphia. And then there was that day in the yellow jersey.

One day, true, but how many support riders in the long history of the Tour de France have worn the jersey even one day?

Armstrong, who is among Yates's biggest supporters, forecast the moment of glory before the Tour started when he was asked about Chris Boardman's chances of wearing the yellow jersey in England.

Indignantly, the American replied: "Who's to say Sean Yates won't be the hero coming home to England? You want to talk about someone who deserves it, he's the one. Chris Boardman is super, but Sean Yates — this is his 12th Tour de France. He's the one who deserves to be the hero, the hero in yellow. As far as people paying their dues, he still pedals his bike as fast and strong as anybody else. He's always the strongest in the team time trial. He kills guys.

"He's probably the most respected guy on our team. There is nobody in the sport, absolutely nobody, that can descend faster. You're talking about big *cojones*."

[STAGE 8]

Attracting Attention

THE CURSE OF THE RAINBOW JERSEY SOUNDS LIKE THE TITLE OF A novel Armstrong might read during a bicycle race, but it isn't. Armstrong insists it was autobiography.

Since he won the rainbow-striped jersey of the world champion, Armstrong had had problems winning again in Europe. Everybody knew who he was now, he said accurately, and nobody would let him make an unaccompanied attack in a race.

"This is always going to attract attention," he said, referring to his jersey. It travels in a crowd, and that's what Armstrong did again in the eighth stage, a 218.5-kilometer slog from Poitiers to Trélissac in the Perigord region of southwestern France.

The American finished 53rd among the 176 riders, and now ranked in eighth place overall, 42 seconds behind the leader; but he had not been able to come close to an individual stage victory.

The rider who finished first that day wore the jersey of the TVM team from the Netherlands. He was Bo Hamburger, an ambitious Dane, who easily pulled away in the last few dozen meters from Angel Camargo, a 27-year-old Colombian with the Spanish squad Kelme. A fine climber, Camargo proved again that there is no such thing as a Colombian sprinter. Third and fourth were their companions in a long breakaway on a scorching day over rolling countryside, the Frenchman Luc Leblanc and German Rolf Aldag. Hamburger was timed in five hours, nine minutes, 27 seconds at a speed of 42.3 kilometers an hour. Camargo was a second slower and the two others four more seconds behind. The pack, including all the overall leaders, finished 2:16 down.

The yellow jersey was retained by Museeuw despite a crash in a village with the sci-fi name of Nontron. Museeuw scrambled up and carried on, protecting a five-second overall lead on Bortolami.

Leblanc, who will never win that scholarship from MIT to study rocket science, was the major victim of the stage. As the leader of the Festina team, he should have been saving himself for the next day's long individual time trial, the first big rendezvous of the Tour after a week of stages meaningless in the big picture. Instead, Leblanc could not resist the temptation to break away in his native region of the Perigord, which was festooned with banners exhorting him to *"Allez, Lulu."* Allez he did, going clear at kilometer 106, being joined shortly afterward by his three companions, and helping build a lead that peaked at 7:30.

That was more than enough to put him in the yellow jersey if the breakaway could hold the margin, but it couldn't. Leblanc was 3:20 behind the man in the yellow jersey at the start of the stage and succeeded only in reducing that by 2:16, which lifted him to 14th place overall, while exhausting himself. And, because Aldag picked up more bonus seconds than Leblanc in sprints along the way, if the breakaway had gained more than 3:20 it would have been the German who donned the jersey, not Leblanc.

Allez Lulu, indeed. As Armstrong could have told him, an eye-catching jersey brings nothing but grief.

Unlike Leblanc, the American had his mind on the next day's stage, hoping to improve in the time trial. The 64-kilometer race against the clock was, Armstrong said, "a little bit long for me. I've never done a time trial that long."

"I'm excited," he continued. "Obviously I'm not going to win, but I'm going to do 100 percent. I feel I have good form, so I'm interested to see where it puts me compared to last year." He finished 27th then, more than six minutes behind the winner, Indurain.

"I'm starting two minutes ahead of Indurain this time," Armstrong noted, "so I better go fast. I've got to go really fast" or risk being overtaken, passed and embarrassed in the rainbow jersey.

[STAGE 9]

Into the Rhythm

RIDING WITH HIS ACCUSTOMED POWER, MIGUEL INDURAIN TRASHED the Tour de France pack in the individual time trial and started toward his fourth consecutive victory in the race.

There had been some doubts about the Spaniard's strength and speed … but not to worry. Indurain answered his critics in the initial six kilometers as he clocked the fastest time to that first checkpoint. Then he began gathering speed.

Barely 10 kilometers later, he had overhauled the rider who started two minutes before him, Armstrong. Other victims began turning up regularly in Indurain's wake. At the end of the 64-kilometer time trial from Perigueux to Bergerac in the extremely hospitable Perigord region, the carnage was nearly total.

Indurain finished at least four minutes ahead of all 175 other riders except for his main rival, Tony Rominger. And the Swiss was able to limit his loss only to a big two minutes.

The winner was timed in one hour, 15 minutes, 58 seconds over a demanding course in a stifling heat in the low 90s. An intermittent light breeze did nothing to hinder the riders, but kept tens of thousands of fans along the course from swooning.

"Despite the heat, I tried to do my maximum and I think I succeeded," said Indurain, who can understate almost as well as he can time trial. His face impassive, he gulped water from a big bottle once across the line and then continued, "I think we have the team to defend the jersey."

He was now wearing the yellow jersey with a 2:28 advantage on Rominger, with French hope Armand De Las Cuevas of Castorama, third, 4:40 behind. Thereafter the numbers belonged to astronomy.

In the time trial, De Las Cuevas finished third with a deficit of 4:22; De Las Cuevas's teammate Thierry Marie was fourth, 4:45 behind; and prologue winner Boardman was fifth, 5:27 behind. Boardman was in seventh place overall.

Looking wan, Rominger paid the obvious tribute: "I have to admit that Indurain was stronger today." Rominger, who had spurts of bad luck in 1993, when he finished second to Indurain in the Tour, had a flat tire a bit less than halfway through this time trial and lost perhaps 30 seconds in having his wheel changed.

Wearily referring to his two-minute deficit, he said, "I'll have to see if I can make it up in the mountains." The Tour would enter the Pyrénées in two days, and the Alps nearly a week later. Although there would probably be many challenges and surprises before then, Indurain answered the big question in the time trial. He regained his rhythm, he said, in the first eight stages of the Tour.

The tall Spaniard demonstrated that rhythm as he rode along a twisty backcountry road that had several patches of melted tar. Up the gradual climbs and down the sinuous descents went Indurain, his body immobile from the waist up to reduce resistance, his face set in concentration, his line of attack through the many turns always tight. His power and speed were plain to see. At the 15-kilometer checkpoint, he led Rominger by 55 seconds, De Las Cuevas by 1:02 and Boardman by 1:36.

The lead increased by the next checkpoint, at kilometer 29.8, where Rominger was 1:23 behind, De Las Cuevas at 1:59 and Boardman at 2:28. The road became gentler after that, its curves tamed and its surface smoother. Indurain kept pounding and caught and passed De Las Cuevas with 10 kilometers to go.

An earlier casualty of the Indurain flypast, Armstrong finished in 13th place, 6:23 down. He was hoping to monitor his development in the race against the clock since the last Tour and the finding was mixed: The year before he lost 6:04 to winner Indurain, but finished 27th.

Farther down the list was Leblanc. After rashly expending his energy on an unsuccessful breakaway the day before, the Frenchman finished 26th in the time trial, 8:04 down, and now ranked 16th overall. Possibly, he believed all the hooey about Indurain's loss of dominance and thought the time trial would be close.

[STAGE 10]
The Morning After

ANYBODY PLANNING TO FORM A MIGUEL INDURAIN FAN CLUB, please remember to send a membership application to Lance Armstrong.

"Big Mig!" the American exclaimed the morning after the time trial. "Too much! The man is just too strong."

That was the consensus throughout the Tour de France pack, which continued to talk about nothing except the Spaniard's show of force. "He's untouchable," said Jim Ochowicz, Motorola's general manager. "He dominated the pack and you have to wonder whether anybody still thinks he can be beaten."

By wiping out the field, Indurain demonstrated that he had regained the form that has led to his previous three successive victories in the Tour. His methodology is always the same — win the first long race against the clock by a big margin, cow his rivals, and then stay with them in the mountains.

"I don't think Rominger will be able to lose him in the mountains," Armstrong continued.

But, while Indurain had already won the 81st Tour in the group consciousness, the rules were somewhat rigid and insisted that he could not be crowned until the finish in Paris, nearly two weeks off. So the Tour continued, with stage 10 moving 160.5 scenic kilometers from Bergerac to Cahors in the southwest.

And — surprise! surprise! — a rider from the home country put *France* back in the Tour de France: Jacky Durand of the Castorama team was the first Frenchman in this race to climb to the victory podium. To the cheers of tens of thousands of his fellow citizens, Durand, waving gleefully, cruised across the line alone.

The stage was raced in three hours, 38 minutes, 11 seconds — a rapid 44.1 kilometers an hour on a steamy day without a wisp of wind. An Italian, Marco Serpellini of Lampre, was second, 55 seconds later, and an Australian, Stephen Hodge of Festina, was third, four more seconds behind.

Durand's victory was deserved since he, wearing the blue-white-and-red jersey of the French national champion, had attacked often during the Tour. Otherwise the nearly three dozen French riders had not been quite so — how do you say it? — *energetique*.

Their lack of results mirrored the French performance in the previous year's Tour, when they scored just one stage victory, and the highest placed rider overall was only 15th. No French rider had won the Tour since 1985 and none had been on the final three-man podium since 1989. In all, it had been a dismal year for French athletes, who left the Winter Olympic Games with just one silver medal and four bronzes, were blanked in their own Grand Slam tennis tournament, and failed even to qualify for soccer's World Cup tournament in the United States.

No wonder, then, that Durand's victory stirred the crowd in Cahors.

The pack appeared 1:55 after the victor and there was just one change in the main overall standings as Bortolami moved from fourth place to third. Bortolami finished fifth on the stage after a long four-man breakaway was ignored in the heat by all save three chasers.

Indurain looked serene in the yellow jersey. "The Extraterrestrial," proclaimed *L'Équipe*, using the word first applied to him by a rival, Gianni Bugno, after the Spaniard overwhelmed the pack in the first time trial of the 1992 Tour.

Armstrong could vouch for the description.

"He just killed me, blew my head off," said the American, who in the previous day's time trial was passed after 16 of the 64 kilometers. "I knew he'd catch me, but I didn't think he'd do it so soon."

Armstrong was equally impressed by the Spaniard's seeming lack of effort: "I was up out of my saddle, really working … and Indurain was sitting down. Calm. I tried to stay with him and did for a while, but then I just couldn't. He was going at 53 Ks."

At the finish, when he was still strong enough to sprint for the line, Indurain was traveling a bit slower. His speed averaged 50.5 kph, about as fast as a car could travel safely on the narrow and curving road.

[STAGE 11]

"Rominger is Dead"

HALFWAY UP THE FIRST BIG CLIMB IN THE 81ST TOUR, INDURAIN looked back once over his left shoulder and then once over his right. When he saw that his major rival, Rominger, had been left behind, Indurain knew just what he had to do — attack.

He gave the order to his teammate Jean-François Bernard, who was leading the climb: "Rominger is dead," Indurain said. "Go." Twenty minutes later, the Spaniard rode out of a thick screen of cold mist and crossed the finish line after another terrible show of force. For the second time in the week, following his victory in the time trial, he had exploded the race.

Indurain badly wanted to win the 11th stage, the first of two in the Pyrénées … but did not. He was left two seconds behind in the final few hundred meters by Leblanc — the second French winner in two days — and had to settle for second place among the 175 riders who started the 263.5-kilometer stage from Cahors to Lour des-Hautacam, a mountaintop ski resort.

Indurain did, however, succeed in nearly doubling his lead — to a huge 4:47 over Rominger in second place. De Las Cuevas was still third, 5:36 behind; Piotr Ugrumov, a Latvian with Gewiss-Ballan, was fourth, 8:32 behind; and Leblanc was now fifth, at 8:35.

Although the finish in Paris was still 11 days away and many big mountains remained, there could not be a rider left who believed that Indurain could be denied his fourth consecutive victory.

Leblanc was timed in six hours, 58 minutes, 4 seconds, a fast pace of 37.8 kilometers an hour considering the length of the stage and the steepness of the final climb — which was rated beyond category on the standard scale of one, hardest, to four, easiest. The speed would probably have been lower in hotter weather, but the riders had a comfortable day in the 70s under overcast and sometimes drizzly skies.

Following the second-placed Indurain was Marco Pantani, a talented Italian climber with Carrera-Tassoni, 18 seconds behind the winner. Frenchman Richard Virenque of Festina, another climber, was fourth, at 56 seconds, and De Las Cuevas was fifth, 58 seconds behind.

Among the day's more noteworthy casualties were Boardman and Claudio Chiappucci. The exhausted Boardman had to quit his first Tour de France; and the sick Chiappucci, who had set his heart on winning here, finished 168th, nearly 24 minutes behind. Now in 135th place overall, Chiappucci, who had completed the Tour in as high as second and third place in the last four years, would get a chance to recover the next day, the race's single day off in three weeks of competition.

The outlook was bleak for Rominger, too. He had labored on the second half of the 13.6-kilometer ascent to Lourdes-Hautacam and wisely decided to climb at his own pace, rather than blow up while trying to chase the man wearing the yellow jersey with No. 1 pinned to it.

Grimacing with his effort, although he rarely rose from his saddle as the others did, Indurain attacked behind Bernard on grades that ranged up to 10 percent and averaged just under 8 percent. Once he jumped away from his teammate, the nearly dozen riders around him began falling behind.

Pantani had the lead at that point, after he and the other leaders overhauled a five-man breakaway that romped through a good part of the stage before the climb. With 3 kilometers left and a thick bank of fog over the road, Leblanc and Indurain were the Italian's two closest pursuers. As they caught him, one on either side, Leblanc bolted away. The Spaniard fought back, regained his lost 200 meters, and then tried to get away himself.

A rider who has often allowed an opponent to win a stage while he himself widened his overall lead, Indurain this time went for the victory. His focus said so, his determination said so, his speed said so.

Leblanc said no.

Each time Indurain passed him, the Frenchman drew even. On the last curve before the straightaway to the line, he whipped ahead into the fog and was gone. Indurain had run out of road.

❋

THE TOUR WAS ENJOYING, IF THAT WAS THE WORD, ITS ONE DAY OFF. After a training excursion in the hills near Lourdes, Armstrong was sweating as he rode his bicycle on rollers. "On a day like this, it's good to have a sweat, not be completely stagnant," Armstrong more or less grunted.

He was disappointed after the previous day's stage and the first climb of the Tour, he admitted. "I was quite a ways back, like 64th on the day. I felt super on the first 250 kilometers, I was so motivated and ready to go for the climb, but when they went I didn't have the legs to go with them."

That was common on the first climb after so many days on the flat, and even more common among young riders. Armstrong knew that, which is why he could say that he was "a little disappointed in my performance, but I'm not depressed about it. I thought I'd do better but I'm not upset. I realize that's not something I'm really expected to do right now. I have to focus on the things that suit me. I've got to be realistic."

He did not know the Pyrénées and was prepared for a long day in the next stage. "I'm definitely confused about tomorrow, whether I make another effort and try to go with the leaders or whether I realize it's not my time right now and sit back." When would he decide? "At the bottom of the Tourmalet," after the Peyresourde and Aspin climbs, he said with a laugh. "I've shown the ability to climb in instances, but maybe I'm not suited for that. It's fine. I'll ride the classics the rest of my life. If I never develop into the Tour rider some think I can be, the climber that some think I can be…." That thought he left unfinished.

And — he said as the rollers spun — he was tired.

"A few days ago, I even entertained thoughts of finishing this Tour, but I'm tired. I hate to start something and stop, but in this situation I think it's better to stop when you're not too tired. I have to realize my goals later in the year. There's no sense killing yourself here just for a finish.

"But at the same time I stopped last year, and this year…. Still, I'm only 22 and that's very young even to start the Tour de France. So I can see Montpellier the last day, maybe Carpentras, maybe the Ventoux if I'm feeling better."

In this mood, Armstrong was sympathetic toward Boardman, who had quit during the Hautacam stage. "Riders who are sick and struggling, they should stop. You don't have much control over the variables in the sport: You get bad weather and you get bronchitis, you eat bad food and you get sick, you crash and break a bone. Whatever. It's a hard sport. A lot of things can go wrong that are completely out of your control."

[STAGE 12]

Victory for Virenque

ANOTHER FRENCHMAN, THIS TIME VIRENQUE OF THE FESTINA TEAM, won his country's third successive stage; Indurain widened his overall lead again; and Rominger faltered once more. So what was new in the Tour?

What was new was unhappy: For the first time in his six years in the race,

Chiappucci, the feisty Italian who had finished second, third, second and sixth since 1990, had to drop out. Because of a high fever that had weakened him, Chiappucci was unable to sign in for the start of the 204.5-kilometer stage through the Pyrénées.

El Diablo, as Chiappucci devilishly likes to style himself with a nickname he picked up in Colombia, would have loved this stage. The weather was ideal — cloudy and not overly hot — and the cheering of hundreds of thousands of fans along the route is what the little man lives for. Plus the mountains. There were three small climbs near the start in Lourdes, three monster climbs farther along, and then a long, steep and exhausting ramp up to the finish in the ski resort of Luz-Ardiden.

Chiappucci loves to climb, to attack on climbs and to win on climbs. In 1992, when he took home the polka-dot jersey as the King of the Mountains, he scored a monumental victory with a long breakaway in the Alps that ended in triumph at Sestriere, in his native Italy. The year before, the stage he won was in the Pyrénées.

But on the 12th stage in 1994, El Diablo was there only in the many paintings of his name across the road, the signs "Allez Chiappi" along the route and the forlorn presence near the finish of a fan, wearing horns on his head and carrying a pitchfork, who turned out daily in the Tour to inspire his hero.

Chiappucci's teammate, roommate and protégé, Pantani, tried to win the stage in homage to the master. But Pantani, 24 years old, did not yet have the bravado of Chiappucci, 31: Although he wanted to be called *El Diablillo*, the little devil, Pantani was usually nicknamed *Il Elefantino* for his jug ears.

Pantani could do no better than second place. Ordinarily, that would have been plenty good enough on such a testing stage; but not this day, not with all the emotion riding with Pantani. His problem was that he waited too long to go on the offense. Virenque got there first.

The Frenchman joined a six-man attack up to the Peyresourde Pass about halfway through the stage and began opening a lead on the climb to a height of 5147 feet. That climb, like the next one, to the Aspin Pass (4885 feet high), was rated first category — one from the worst — in length, steepness and general difficulty.

Building a lead of more than six minutes over the pack, Virenque and his companions stayed together until they were near the top of the Aspin. He attacked there and again on the Tourmalet climb, which followed. Five kilometers from that pass — which stands 6939 feet high and is rated beyond category — he was alone.

Virenque never weakened on the ultimate ramp to Luz-Ardiden, 5626 feet high and also rated beyond category. His face ablaze with joy, the French rider crossed the finish line a crushing 4 minutes 34 seconds ahead of Pantani and 5:52 ahead of another Italian, Oscar Pellicioli of Polti, in third place.

Virenque's performance vaulted him from 29th place, 15:38 behind Indurain, to third overall, 7:56 down. Rominger remained in second place with the same 7:56 deficit, up from 4:47 that morning. He finished 17th in the stage, 10:51 behind Virenque.

The general toll was immense. Four riders, including Chiappucci, did not start and eight others dropped out en route, reducing the original 189 riders to 161, with four days in the Alps still ahead. Armstrong finished 55th, at 20:09.

To the immense cheers of tens of thousands of Spanish, particularly Basque, spectators, Indurain was awarded a fresh yellow jersey. He had been paced regally by his Banesto teammates until halfway up the final climb, when the Spaniard went to the front himself and pumped away for sixth place in the stage, 7:42 behind. As expected, he rode defensively against all his rivals in the general classification and did not once attempt to attack.

Nor did he need to with his nearly eight-minute lead. Few things can be certain in a three-week race, however. As Indurain pointed out in a news conference on the Tour's day off, he could wake up sick one morning, just as Rominger and Chiappucci had done. So nobody was preparing a concession speech yet, even if Indurain was the odds-on favorite. As Stephen Roche, the Irishman who won the Tour in 1987 and now traveled with it as a civilian, confusingly put it: "Don't take it as fact that the Tour is over when it's not, although it probably is."

Armstrong was far clearer: "The Tour is over. Miguel Indurain is super right now, Indurain is far superior. The whole duel between Indurain and Rominger was a figment of the media's imagination. That's all created. It was never even a race." He recalled his prediction before the start in Lille that the Indurain-Rominger battle was merely media hype and that Indurain was a certain winner. "I'm getting better at predicting cycling, I am, I think I'm improving," Armstrong said proudly.

"It's a race for second now and I don't think Rominger is going to wind up getting second. I don't think he's guaranteed second. There's a lot more racing to go."

[STAGE 13]

Giving Up

LANCE ARMSTRONG WAS RIGHT. TWO WEEKS TO THE DAY THAT HE started the Tour as most observers' co-favorite, Tony Rominger coasted to the side of the road, surrendered his rider's number and dropped out of the race.

Although the official explanation by his Mapei-CLAS team was gastroenteritis, the unofficial and more widely believed cause was total loss of morale. Rominger denied this later. "I have a problem," he said in a calm and flat voice at a news conference. "I've had the problem for three days and today I paid for it. I was over my limit."

Asked if the problem was purely physical, he bristled. "Yes, only physical," he replied testily in his one show of emotion.

The Swiss rider, who was still second overall when he abandoned, had been crushed three times in a week by Indurain. First the Spaniard left his main rival two minutes behind in the first individual time trial. Then he gained 2:19 in the first big climb of the Tour, after which Rominger revealed that he had a stomach ailment. Finally, Indurain added 3:09 in the major stage over the Pyrénées.

The total, including time accrued in other stages, added up to 7:56, which left Rominger discouraged. At a news conference on the race's day off, he said that he had recovered from his illness and that he would carry on to the end in Paris on July 24 — even though he knew he now was in a battle for second, not first, place.

People close to him reported, however, how frail his resolve had become.

Victory in the Tour meant so much to Rominger, still the No. 1 rider in computerized rankings of the world's top 800 professionals. The winner of the Vuelta a España in May, the Swiss had even prepared for his challenge to Indurain by traveling to Vail, Colorado, to train at altitude for three weeks in June.

When he quit, he was struggling behind the pack about two thirds of the way through the 223-kilometer stiflingly hot and humid stage from Bagnères-de-Bigorre in the Pyrénées to the splendid red-brick city of Albi in the Midi.

"I can't remember what I was thinking about when I quit," Rominger said later, replying to a question at his news conference.

"Disappointment is hard," he said in French, one of a half-dozen languages he speaks. "My disappointment is too hard to explain," he added in English. He said that he had not cried.

A Danish rider, Bjarne Riis of Gewiss-Ballan, won the stage by leaving behind a seven-man breakaway 11 kilometers from the finish and then holding off all 158 other riders to coast home free by nine seconds. His time of five hours, 14 minutes, 48 seconds, an average speed of 42.5 kilometers an hour, was harder than a person should have to work in such a heat wave. Svorada won the pack sprint for second place, and Abdujaparov was third.

Indurain continued to wear the overall leader's yellow jersey by 7:56 over Virenque. De Las Cuevas was third, 8:02 behind.

The day was Indurain's 30th birthday and he celebrated before the stage by posing, in an annual ritual, with a big cake as platoons of photographers, in another annual ritual, trod on well-wishers.

The big question for his Banesto teammates was a suitable gift. What do you give a man who is paid $2 million a year and who has a lovely wife, a supportive family and seemingly not a care in the world? A necktie would not do, since Indurain already owns one.

So the team gave him a restful day. Surrounding their leader at the front of the pack, the Banestos rode a steady and high tempo to curb breakaways and let Indurain travel along blithely in their slipstream. From the corn and wheat fields of the Pyrénées to the serious sunflower territory of the Midi, Indurain remained untroubled, the birthday boy in the yellow jersey. It happens every July 16.

[STAGE 14]

The End of Another Star

LOOKING DRAWN AND STUNNED, GIANNI BUGNO SAT AT A TABLE in Castres and tried to explain why he would not be starting the 14th stage in a few minutes. No spark, said Bugno, the Italian who finished second in the Tour in 1991 and who won the world road-race championship that same year and the year after.

No spark, the leader of the Polti team repeated wearily, no legs and no ambition. He had suffered enough since the Tour began. He could see no point in continuing for the final week, including four days of climbing in the Alps.

That same morning, Belgian rider Edwig Van Hooydonck of WordPerfect and Spanish rider Roberto Sierra of ONCE did not call news conferences to explain why they were not starting. The continuing heat wave, with temperatures reaching 93 degrees Fahrenheit, and the rapidity of the daily stages were explanation enough.

"I'm fried," complained Armstrong. "Totally fried."

He turned to a Motorola teammate, Stephen Swart of New Zealand. "You fried?" Armstrong asked.

"I was fried a *week* ago," Swart replied.

"And I couldn't sleep last night," Armstrong continued in his litany of woe. "Too hot. I fell asleep finally about 1 a.m. and then woke up soaked in sweat at 5." His agony was scheduled to end the next day, when he was expected to drop out of the Tour, just before the Alps, to save his strength for the defense of his world championship title in August.

Unlike 15 of the 159 riders who started the 202-kilometer stage from Castres to Montpellier, Armstrong and Swart made it to the finish. Each trailed in with the pack, 5:56 behind, as a five-man breakaway was allowed to lead the Tour eastward through the steamy and enthusiastic Languedoc region.

In a cat-and-mouse duel during the last kilometer, GB-MG's Sørensen edged Australian Neil Stephens of ONCE. Sørensen, the better sprinter, slowed and waited until Stephens dashed for the line, then came around him to record the second successive Danish victory.

Two of the leaders' accomplices in the breakaway came in 1:13 later: Rolf Järmann, a Swiss teammate of Sørensen, was third, followed by an Italian, Massimo Ghirotto of ZG-Selle Italia. Fifth, two more seconds behind, was Frenchman Pascal Hervé of Festina.

The pack, controlled by Indurain's Banesto team, was content to have five riders low in the time standings maintain a big lead and thus discourage other attacks. Sørensen, for example, started the day in 48th place overall, 34:29 behind Indurain, and Stephens was 85th, 55:53 behind. When the overall leaders finished 5:56 after them, the Dane rose only to 40th place and the Australian to 64th among the 141 riders left. Indurain continued in the yellow jersey by 7:56 over Virenque.

In the language of professional cycling, this was termed a transitional stage because it led from one set of mountains, the Pyrénées, to another. Although a transitional stage is usually full of incident but not casualties, this one was chockablock with them.

As early as the first climb, amid cattle pastures and fields stacked with rolls of hay, riders began falling behind. The climb up the Côte de la Fontesse was 9 kilometers long, true, and rated second category, but the gradient was only 5 percent. The action was led by Peter De Clercq, a Belgian with Lotto who wore the polka-dot jersey of best climber for the Tour's first nine days by piling up points on similarly small climbs. He was as much King of the Mountains, however, as he was king of the Belgians. Once the Tour reached the Pyrenees, he dropped off the charts.

While he regained a few points by topping the rise first and heading into a gentle descent through a fresh-smelling pine forest, the pack was strung out behind him. The noon sun and fatigue were taking their toll. First to quit was an Italian, Mario Scirea of Polti. On the second climb, up the third-category Côte de Combespinasse, De Clercq was nowhere to be seen and more riders began faltering. Christophe Capelle, a Frenchman with GAN, went out of the race and so did Durand, a stage winner a week earlier.

Sixteen riders attacked shortly afterward and the number at the front dwindled to five on the next climb, the third-category Fonfroide Pass. Down the 3182-foot-high hill the five went, leaving behind a hint of coolness at altitude and returning to the furnace of the Agout River's valley.

The Banesto team worked hard to overtake the 11 riders caught between the pack and the leaders, since there was a dangerous rider among them. He was Pantani, who ranked seventh overall and would be a fine climber for the Alps. When the 11 were swallowed up, the breakaway's lead was just two minutes. Once Banesto relaxed, the lead rose to a peak of 11 minutes and the five rode unchallenged and saluted by an immense number of fans along the road. Behind the breakaway, a dozen more riders decided they could not go on.

With 18 kilometers remaining, Stephens attacked. Sørensen was the only one who could stay with him and they worked perfectly together to head for the finish line, the decisive waiting game and then the sprint in this transitional stage.

[STAGE 15]

Kamikaze First Class

THE TOUR DE FRANCE FINALLY SLOWED, PEDALING AT A LANGUID 25 kilometers an hour from the start, because the riders were intimidated by the one bump in the road ahead. And what a bump that was: Mont Ventoux, a climb rated beyond category. Mont Ventoux, a barren mountaintop of scorching heat. And the day was already hot. Rising 6263 feet from the plains of the Vaucluse region, the mountain lay hidden in a heat haze generated by another day of high humidity and temperatures in the mid-90s.

Even in moderate weather, the Ventoux was known as a terrifying climb — 21 kilometers long on a grade of more than 8 percent for 16 kilometers and nearly 10 percent for the rest. Despite its name of Windy Mountain, it is often without a trace of fresh air in the summer. For nearly the last half of the climb, it is without a trace of shade.

Was Eros Poli intimidated? Poli, kamikaze first class? "I have to keep trying to do something if I want to win a stage," the Italian rider for the Mercatone Uno team said, a few days after he set off on a long and unsuccessful solo attack on the seventh stage, to Futuroscope. "So I'll keep trying."

When he tried this day, nobody responded by chasing him and probably a few in the pack laughed. A support rider who leads the team's sprinters — notably the esteemed Mario Cipollini — into the final few hundred meters, Poli was not a winner and certainly not a climber.

Let them laugh. The next time a rider saw Poli it was four-and-a-half hours later and he was standing on the victory podium in Carpentras, waving gleefully at a huge crowd.

After a brave and imaginative ride alone for 171 kilometers, the Italian finished first by 3:39, down from a peak of nearly 24 minutes. Second was Italian Alberto Elli of GB-MG, and third was Frenchman Pascal Lino of Festina, both in the same deficit.

Most of the overall leaders were far ahead of the main pack and Indurain, who finished ninth, remained in the yellow jersey by 7:56 over Virenque, who finished fifth.

Of the 189 riders who started on July 2, just 135 remained — after two more quit during the stage and three, including Armstrong, did not start. Another casualty was Rob Harmeling, a Dutch sprinter with TVM, who was disqualified late the night before for getting up a climb by holding onto his team car. The penalty was meant as a warning for the mountainous days ahead.

The pack, which had been tearing along furiously all other days, rode slowly from the start of the 15th stage. Two hours after the departure in Montpellier, nobody had yet attacked and the speed remained a constant 25 kph.

Mont Ventoux's peak sat at kilometer 190.5 of the 231-kilometer stage and the climb began at kilometer 172. What rider could be in a hurry to get there?

Järmann could. The Swiss broke the truce by attacking a bit beyond kilometer 48. Quickly reeled in by the pack's first acceleration of the day, he was followed on the offensive by Davide Cassani, an Italian teammate, and Polti's Fidanza. Although they were quickly caught, too, the burst of speed left several riders behind. With four days of climbing in the Alps ahead, starting the next day, the riders seemed to want no more reductions in the ranks. They resumed their slow march.

That was too much of a challenge for Poli. After his long — 166 kilometers, four hours — and unsuccessful solo attack on the way to Futuroscope, he explained his motives in addition to his quest for victory: "If I don't attack, I have nothing to do." He had found himself without a Mercatone Uno sprinter to lead because Cipollini was sick and not competing and another, Baffi, quit early in the Tour.

So, on a wretchedly hot and humid day, Poli went away and stayed away, riding alone through a landscape without people or villages for mile after mile. His only view was the road ahead and the vineyards on either side of it.

Through the Gard region he went, past vineyards that produce a fair table wine (Côtes du Gard), as his lead began mounting from seconds to minutes. By the time he reached the upmarket vineyards of Châteauneuf du Pape, his lead was 10:16.

Pushed by a tail wind as he passed a Roman viaduct in the first of two transits of Carpentras, Poli was cruising 20:35 ahead of the pack and 15:50 ahead of his only chaser, Mario Montavan, an Italian with Carrera. The lead over the pack attained a peak of nearly 24 minutes just after Poli reached yet more vineyards, those for Côtes du Ventoux, another fair table wine, and first spotted the mountain.

Poli went at it with gusto, rising from his saddle as the road ascended and defying the blazing sun by removing the visor he wears instead of the usual cap. Mont Ventoux fought back. On another suffocating July day in 1967, it was the scene of the only death in the modern Tour — that of Englishman Tom Simpson, who succumbed to heat exhaustion exacerbated by amphetamines.

A memorial marker to Simpson is placed where he fell, a kilometer from the top amid baked chips of limestone. Tour officials and such star riders from the past as Eddy Merckx and Bernard Hinault placed a bouquet there minutes before

Poli struggled by.

The big Italian was haggard by then, wearing a tormented stare and black around his eyes. "I think I lost 5 kilos (11 pounds) on the climb," he said later. He was still climbing though, at Simpson's memorial, and was seven minutes ahead of the awakened pack.

At the peak, the Italian's lead was down to 4:31 on his nearest pursuer and 6:03 over the group that included Indurain and Virenque.

Getting up was the hard part for Poli, who stands 6 feet 4 inches and weighs 190 pounds. Descending was far easier, and he maintained most of his lead for the final 40 kilometers to the line.

As he neared it, he drank often from his water bottle and then squirted the back of his neck. Just before the finish, he broke into a big smile, waved his visor at the fans and somehow made a sweeping bow while pedaling.

[STAGE 16]

King for a Day

ROBERTO CONTI, A VETERAN ITALIAN RIDER WHO HAD NEVER WON A race before, captured the jewel of the Tour's climbing stages and helped shake up the overall standings as the race completed the first of four stages in the Alps, those splendors of nature.

Conti crossed the line at the ski resort of L'Alpe d'Huez an impressive two minutes ahead of the next rider. That moved him up the ranks from 11th place to sixth, and seemed to give him a fighting chance to finish second overall, the only big battle left.

Conti, who rides for the Lampre team, was ecstatic about his performance. "It's a great victory for me," he said. Nevertheless, he continued, he understood that he was a support rider and would return to that role, working for the team and not himself, in the mountainous days to come.

But Conti would have something to remember when he was following orders. The Alpe d'Huez stage, with its long and steep rise up 21 switchbacks, usually attracts an enormous number of spectators, perhaps a quarter of a million, and is the day all climbers spend the winter dreaming about.

His strategy was simple. Conti slipped into an early 14-man breakaway that built a lead of more than eight minutes over two mountains rated second category. Then, out of the low clouds that shrouded the Alps as the weather finally turned cool, there stood Alpe d'Huez, rated beyond category. On the many twists of its 13.8-kilometer climb, Conti disposed of his companions.

In second place was a Colombian, Hernan Buenahora of Kelme-Avianca. Third, 3:49 behind the winner, was German Udo Bölts of Telekom, in the same time as the Italian Elli, who was fourth.

Despite the turn in the weather, attrition continued to be a factor. Of the 189 riders who started the Tour, just 128 remained. Seven more dropped out on the way to Alpe d'Huez, victims of fatigue brought on by a heat wave and the race's rapid pace.

Conti was timed in six hours, 6 minutes, 45 seconds, an average of 36.7 kilometers an hour over the 224.5 kilometers from Valréas in the flatlands to L'Alpe d'Huez in the stratosphere.

On the way there, Indurain lost 35 seconds of his huge lead. It was now down to 7:21 over Virenque, who came in 11th, just ahead of the Spaniard. Indurain looked strong and untroubled moving up to the 6102-foot-high peak. On a speedy descent from Mont Ventoux the previous day, the race leader nearly went over the edge of the mountain when his brakes locked and his front wheel skidded, so the loss of 35 seconds had to be taken in perspective.

Besides Conti, the day's gainers included Leblanc, who rose from fourth place to third; Pantani, who rose from sixth place to fifth, and Elli, who rose from 13th place to eighth. Those on the down staircase included De Las Cuevas, who fell from third place to fourth; Vladimir Pulnikov, a Ukrainian with Carrera, who fell from fifth place to seventh, and Abraham Olano, a Spaniard with Mapei-CLAS, who fell from 10th place to 16th.

The main losers on the day, however, may have been the Dutch fans of professional bicycle racing. They usually flock to L'Alpe d'Huez, camping overnight in its meadows, for a chance to cheer on their countrymen. And Dutch climbers have often responded with victories.

Not lately, though, and surely not this day. Erik Breukink, who rides for ONCE, was the first Dutchman to cross the line, in 47th place, 13:44 behind Conti. Since that placing was not unexpected and since two of the few other Dutch climbers of note, Steven Rooks and Gert-Jan Theunisse, both of the TVM team, dropped out in the Pyrénées, many Dutch fans went elsewhere on vacation.

The long road up to L'Alpe d'Huez was strangely devoid of the red-white-and-blue bands of the Dutch flag, and the encouraging cry of "Hup, hup" was rarely heard. On the other hand, for once there were few rowdies in the crowd and the riders had a clear passage to the finish.

[STAGE 17]

Little Mig

MEET LITTLE MIG ... MIGUEL ARROYO, WHO HAD MORE THINGS IN common with Miguel Indurain — Big Mig — than were apparent at first. Both climb well, for example, both said they were in exemplary form, both put on their bicycling shorts one leg at a time and both were hopeful in the Tour de France.

Abrupt end of similarities. Indurain stands 6 foot 2 inches and weighs 176 pounds; Arroyo is 5 feet 5 inches and 132 pounds. Also, Indurain is Spanish and Arroyo is Mexican.

Then there was the fact that Indurain was leading the Tour by 7:21 and, barring accident or illness, was cruising toward his fourth consecutive victory in the race, while Arroyo ranked 48th and was looking for his first victory of the year.

The two continued on their separate trajectories on the 149-kilometer stage from Bourg d'Oisans, at the foot of L'Alpe d'Huez, to Val Thorens, a mountain-top resort in the Alps. The man in the yellow jersey finished fifth and Arroyo was 92nd, after climbs over the Glandon and Madeleine Passes, both rated first cat-egory, and then up to lofty Val Thorens, rated beyond category ... and no picture postcard either.

In a sprint finish, the winner was a Colombian, Nelson Rodriguez of ZG-Selle Italia, who nipped Gewiss-Ballan's Ugrumov, a Latvian. They were two of three riders who broke away on the Madeleine climb and built a comfortable lead before ditching their accomplice, stage 13 winner Riis, who rode for teammate Ugru-mov until exhausted. Rodriguez finished the stage, conducted in cold and cloudy weather, three seconds faster than Ugrumov, at an average speed of 28.4 kilometers an hour. Two more fatigued riders dropped out, reducing the field to 126.

Third was the astonishing Pantani who, after crashing early in the stage and con-tinuing with a bloody left knee, again waited too long to launch the counterattack that might have made him a winner. By finishing 1:08 behind Rodriguez, howev-er, he moved up to third place overall from fifth, leapfrogging Frenchmen De Las Cuevas and Leblanc.

Leblanc, who finished 2:40 behind, dropped from third place to fourth. Slumped on the road against his team car, he seemed exhausted at the finish and was quickly wrapped in more clothing against a temperature of 48 degrees. De Las Cuevas, who finished 20:02 behind, fell from fourth place to the oblivion of 17th.

As for Indurain, looking invincible as he led a small group's chase up the final mountain after Pantani, he lost no time to the second-placed Virenque, who osten-tatiously sprinted past Indurain to the line to finish fourth. Later, Virenque — who wore the polka-dot jersey of King of the Mountains — explained that he was getting back at the man in the yellow jersey for contesting a climbing bonus. How could Indurain have dared!

Virenque now led Pantani by 50 seconds overall and must have been worrying about the battle for second place. Still more than seven minutes up after this 17th of 21 stages, Big Mig had little to worry about.

"He's incredible," Little Mig said of Indurain. "The big boss, for sure."

The 27-year-old Arroyo was a boss himself for the low-budget Chazal-MBK team, which was allowed into the Tour as a concession to French cycling interests. At the last moment, Tour organizers relaxed their rules limiting the race to 20 teams to let Chazal ride. The team had yet to record a top-five finish in a daily stage, but did rank 12th among the 21 teams in standings based on total accumulated time.

"The team is good," Arroyo said, "pretty good. It's no big team, but for me that's good because I can be the leader. With this team I have more chances to do very good results. And that gives me confidence that I will do good results. I feel happy, I feel good, my condition is much better since the start of the Tour," he continued, smiling often and broadly. "In six years as a professional, I never rode the Tour de France before, so it's difficult.

"Every day is like a classic, long hard stages. It's very difficult, but I feel good and I have good morale. In Mexico, everybody is watching the Tour de France on television, watching Raúl Alcalá and me." Alcalá, who rode for Motorola and was regarded as the better climber of the two, finished 25:54 behind in the stage, the same as Arroyo. Ranked 76th to his countryman's 48th, Alcalá had been struggling throughout and could have used a splash of the pep Arroyo displays.

"I need to do something in the mountains," Arroyo said. "The first part of the Tour, all those little hills, was no good for me. The real hills, that's good for me."

The Mexican's reputation rested on his climbing skills. He was first brought to Europe by Greg LeMond in 1989, on the advice of LeMond's masseur and confidante, Otto Jácome, to work for the ADR team. Arroyo moved with LeMond to the Z team in 1990 and 1991, rode for GB in 1992 and for Subaru the next year. Subaru, which was based in the United States, was invited to the 1993 Tour as a shared entry with the Chazal team Arroyo now rode for. Rejecting the invitation as an affront and vowing to qualify on its own in 1994, Subaru decided instead to go out of the bicycle-racing business during the winter.

It might have made the race as a whole entry the previous year, but Arroyo and Atle Kvalsvoll, the team's best climbers, were both injured in a crash while near the front in the Classique des Alpes in the spring. Neither could have competed in the Tour, which may have influenced the organizers' decision to pair Subaru with Chazal.

While Arroyo steered clear of the many crashes in this Tour, he had other problems, and did not excel in the Pyrénées. On the first climb there, he had a flat and fell behind the leading group to finish 56th, 6:21 down on the winner. The next day, over four massive climbs, he finished 52nd, nearly 20 minutes behind. Going over Mont Ventoux in Provence, Arroyo improved to 36th place, 9:59 behind. He sank back to 50th place, 14:36 behind at the finish atop L'Alpe d'Huez. His performance there rated an asterisk, however, since his rear wheel jammed near the end and he had to walk the disabled bicycle a few hundred yards before he got a replacement.

"I'm tired," he said the next morning, "tired but still trying. Maybe today I can do something, maybe sometimes in the Alps."

Two stages remained in those mountains and, Arroyo kept hoping, *mañana* would be another day.

[STAGE 18]

Lessons Learned

PIOTR URGUMOV LEARNED HIS LESSON ... AND SO DID INDURAIN and Virenque ... as the Tour completed its third stage in the Alps, climbing three big mountains and preparing them for the individual time trial that would decide who would stand second and third below Indurain when the race ended in Paris.

Ugrumov intruded into the handful of contenders by racing away to an easy victory on the 18th stage, a 174.5-kilometer jaunt from Moûtiers to Cluses. A day after he was beaten for victory in a two-man sprint, Ugrumov had the sense to ride alone to the finish. And by completing the stage 2:39 ahead of the second-placed Indurain, the Latvian jumped from sixth place overall to third.

Indurain similarly profited from the previous day's experience of being overtaken in the meaningless sprint for fourth place by Virenque. In the same *mano a mano*, Big Mig turned on the burners this time and left Virenque a second behind.

Eating dust or not, Virenque was content with third place for the stage. He tightened his hold on second place overall, by finishing 45 seconds ahead of his main rival, Pantani, who fell to fourth place from third.

Although there was plenty of climbing, the last 20 kilometers from the 5292-foot-high peak of the Colombière were all downhill. Virenque used that terrain to pull away from the Italian, who is too light at 123 pounds to be an overly speedy descender and has to ride nearly flat, with his butt protruding far behind the saddle, to make the most aerodynamic gain.

So, with the 47.5-kilometer uphill time trial facing the Tour's remaining 119 riders, Indurain was secure in the overall lead by 7:22 over Virenque, who was 1:33 ahead of Urgumov, who was two seconds ahead of Pantani, who was 32 seconds ahead of Leblanc.

Leblanc, who has the suicidal habit of attacking and wasting his energy the day before a time trial, was at it again on this stage. Twice he bolted away and twice he was caught, before he flatted on the final descent and lost enough time to fall from fourth place overall to fifth. Other casualties included the six riders who quit during the day and De Las Cuevas, who ranked as high as third at the beginning of the week. Suffering with a heavy chest cold and demoted to 17th place overall, he did not start the proceedings.

He missed something.

A few puffy clouds in a pale blue sky, a healing sun, a cooling breeze: What a grand day it was for a picnic or a bicycle race, and what a grander day for both together.

Acting on that theory, Constant Pointet, a worker in a charcoal factory, and his apprentice fiancée, Denise Grundet, a cleaning woman, drove up toward the Saisies Peak, 5357 feet high and the first of the three first-category climbs in the stage. Parking their car below a cow pasture full of mauve wildflowers, choosing a spot with a view of the climbing riders through willow and fir trees and unpacking a table, two chairs and a hamper of food and wine, the couple settled down for a festive day.

They were doing exactly what hundreds of thousands of people did this day in the Alps and what millions did around the country during the three weeks of the Tour.

The couple saw only a small part of the stage, of course. As they passed the paté, the slices of ham, the crusty bread, the pickles and the red wine between them, they saw the pack pursuing the first of many breakaways. Belgium's De Clercq and Italy's Cassani were the fugitives on that first climb. After they were caught, dozens of other riders gave it a whirl.

All through the afternoon, the pack was in such a frisky mood that even such dormant teams as Motorola and Novémail had riders in attacks. Ugrumov made his winning move on the second climb, the Croix-Fry Pass, 4813 feet high and populated by lawless hooligans who hurled buckets of water into reporters' cars preceding the riders.

On the final climb, the Latvian rode fast enough to make certain he had no companion to snatch away his victory. Arms aloft in solitary glory, he cruised in just about the time Pointet and Grundet, that happy couple, would have been taking a glass of Pastis as an aperitif for dinner.

[STAGE 19]

Even Indurain Gets Tired

THEY STRUCK THE FRENCH FLAG AND RAISED THE LATVIAN.
To general astonishment, Ugrumov rode to victory in the second individual time trial and rose to a secure second place overall, replacing Virenque, two days before the race ended in Paris.

Ugrumov completed a remarkable three days in the Alps: On the 17th stage, he finished second in a two-man final sprint and beat on his handlebars in frustration; on the 18th stage, he finished first after a solo breakaway; and on the 19th, he overwhelmed the field in a mountainous race against the clock.

His was a victory à la Indurain: one minute 38 seconds faster than Pantani in second place, a vast 3:16 over Big Mig himself in third place, and 3:50 over Leblanc in fourth. Nobody else among the 119 riders finished within four minutes of Ugrumov. He covered the mainly uphill 47.5 kilometers in one hour, 22 minutes, 59 seconds, in intermittent rain from Cluses to Morzine-Avoriaz. His speed of 34.3 kilometers an hour was rapid over three climbs rated third, second and first category, even if the roads had been dry.

Third overall before this stage, the Latvian now was second, 5:39 behind Indurain. Moving up from fourth place to third was Pantani, who ranked 7:19 behind Indurain. Dropping from second place overall to fifth was Virenque, who had a terrible day and nearly crashed turning a corner. He finished 18th, losing 6:04.

"Time-trialing isn't my thing," Virenque said after he crossed the line in heavy rain. Only 24 years old, he had years to improve, and should be a contender in many Tours to come.

Leblanc, his fellow Frenchman and Festina teammate, rose from fifth place overall to fourth, 10:03 behind Indurain and seven seconds ahead of Virenque. "I'll be happy with fourth place when we reach Paris," said Leblanc, 27, thereby helping to explain his perennial underachievement.

The major mystery at the finish was why Indurain had been beaten by more than three minutes. In the first individual time trial, he beat the since-departed Rominger by two minutes … and the rest of the field by more than four. Ugrumov lost 6:04 there.

It was partly the cold rain, which Indurain detests, he explained later. "I didn't want to take any risks in the descents in the rain," he said. "When I heard about halfway how far ahead Ugrumov was, I just rode at a safe pace."

At a news conference, he also cited a lack of passion in a Tour in which he had iced his fourth consecutive victory more than a week ago. "My motivation isn't the same when I've got the race won," he said, noting that, when he was cruising to easy victory the year before, he lost the second time trial to Rominger.

Fatigue also played a part, Indurain continued. "Like everybody, I'm tired. You don't finish a Tour without feeling tired. But I'm no more tired than usual."

Whatever the reason, Ugrumov was absolutely superior.

He rode steadily, smoothly and, of course, speedily over the first climb, 4.9 kilometers long with a grade of 6.3 percent, and never faltered over the second, 10.7 kilometers long with a grade of 5 percent, or the last, 12.4 kilometers long with a grade of 6.7 percent. He seemed untroubled by the wet roads, the rain running down his face and the tens of thousands of fans screaming encouragement and flapping flags in his way.

After a strong second place to Indurain in the previous year's Giro d'Italia, the 33-year-old Ugrumov expected to have a fine season in 1994. But he broke his collarbone in a crash late in the spring and had been working the last two months to return to form.

Besides the 6:04 by which he trailed in the first time trial, he lost more than six minutes to Indurain in the Pyrénées. Only as the Tour moved through the Alps had the Latvian been able to halve his deficit. But Ugrumov would not get much nearer than 5:39....

[STAGE 20]

One More Stage

RIDING ON DESIRE AND DEDICATION, FRANCIS MOREAU MADE IT through one more Tour de France stage and at last knew that he would finish the race the next day in Paris.

His father would have been pleased. Moreau's 113th place among the 117 remaining riders didn't matter. Nor did the fact that he had not come close to any sort of victory in the Tour, his fourth. All his father hoped was that Moreau would finish the race.

Seriously ill with a cardiac condition, Moreau's father said just before the race started July 2 that if he died before it ended, his son was not to drop out in mourning. "This is what he wanted," said Moreau, a 29-year-old French rider for the GAN team, as he prepared for one of the final stages. His father died on July 9 and Moreau was still riding two weeks later.

When the next-to-last stage, a 208.5-kilometer run from Morzine in the Alps to Lac St. Point in the Jura ended, Moreau was too smart, too tired and too slow to get involved in the sprint finish. He finished 51st. Abdujaparov recorded his second stage victory, edging Svorada in the sprint. Third place went to an Italian, Silvio Martinello of Mercatone Uno.

On a cool and overcast day, the riders refrained from attacks and played such practical jokes as snatching spectators' hats. They do it every year when the end is upon them and the pressure drops.

Although two more riders dropped out en route, there was no change in the overall leadership as the pack finished together at Lac St. Point, a lake that is billed as the world's largest ice-skating rink since it freezes in its entirety — about 10 miles around — every winter. Life along its banks appeared to be less exciting in the summer, a possible reason why an immense crowd turned out to watch the Tour whiz into the finish in the village of Malbuisson, population 400.

First in, first out: The Tour left by train immediately afterward for Euro Disney, the start of the ceremonial spin into Paris. One of those train passengers was Moreau, who hung on to his place fifth from the bottom.

His perseverance was his alone. His GAN teammates, reduced to three of nine riders, could offer no support. Even the Tour's organizers were less than gracious when he could have used assistance. After he rode in a time trial on July 11, he was allowed to fly from western France to his home near St. Quentin, outside Paris, for his father's funeral ... but had to return that night. The rules, which were not bent by the organizers, require riders to sleep with their teams or be eliminated.

Officials were less hard-hearted the other time he faced elimination. When 68 riders, including Moreau, finished too late to make the time cutoff on the 17th stage, in the Alps, they were spared elimination by the judges, who cited an obscure codicil to the rules. In truth, nobody wanted to eliminate more than half the remaining field.

"The mountains are tough for everybody, not just me," Moreau said about that day. "But you've got to get over the mountains."

At 6 feet 2 inches and 160 pounds, he is far too big to be a climber, although Indurain is even bigger and much better in the mountains. But then Indurain was the man who was winning the Tour while Moreau was just trying to finish it.

His talent lies elsewhere. He was world pursuit champion on the track in 1990, fourth in the championships the next year and, little less than a month after the Tour, would win the silver medal behind Chris Boardman. Moreau is also a specialist in prologues and a dab hand at the long solo breakaway, as he proved in winning Paris-Brussels the year before.

His experience solo on the road came in handy, since each of the three remaining GAN riders had to look out for himself first. "I'm not alone," Moreau said, "but I don't have much support." Illness, fatigue and crashes reduced the roster, including the two stars, LeMond and Boardman. Building on youth and Boardman's potential, the team would be reorganized for the next year, with LeMond and a few other veterans not invited back.

Since he celebrated his 29th birthday four days before the Tour ended, Moreau might have been considered an endangered veteran. He wasn't though. "His courage is very moving," a GAN official said.

The rider phrased it differently: "Yes, it's for my father," he said. "He was a big fan of cycling and a big fan of mine. It's been a very hard Tour but here I still am." Now, on to Paris.

[STAGE 21]

Still on Top

MIGUEL INDURAIN RODE INTO PARIS IN TRIUMPH, CELEBRATING — IF that is the word — his fourth consecutive victory in the Tour de France.

Just two other riders had recorded four consecutive victories since the race began in 1903. Only those two, Jacques Anquetil and Eddy Merckx, plus Bernard Hinault, had ever won it five times. His latest victory elevated Indurain, at 30, closer to the level of the sport's greatest champions.

"Only the Tour counts," he said in an interview a few days before the finish.

"Every race that comes before it is merely my preparation for the Tour. It will be my major goal again next year."

Despite suspicions in the late spring that he was declining, Indurain finished first by his greatest margin yet. In 1991, Bugno was second by 3:36; in 1992, Chiappucci was second by 4:35; in 1993, Rominger was second by 4:59. This day, the man on the second step of the victory podium, Ugrumov, trailed by 5:39.

Traditionally, the overall leaders do not contest the final stage and this time they were not given a chance to be so gracious. In a rare breakaway on the Champs-Elysées, Eddy Seigneur, one of the survivors on the much-depleted GAN team, caught and overtook American Frankie Andreu (Motorola) in the final 150 meters and won easily as his exhausted opponent slumped on his handlebars. Because his legs felt good, Andreu had jumped away from a five-man break, including Seigneur, with about half-a-mile to go, and held his lead through the Place de la Concorde and part of the final straightaway. Then Seigneur, a strong finisher and one of the brightest hopes of French cycling, came charging by.

In the midst of the trailing pack rode Indurain, who had no more to prove. "I have nothing to say to those who announced my decline," he remarked at a news conference when his final victory was assured. "I already answered them during the race."

Bugno, Chiappucci and Rominger all started the 81st Tour and all withdrew before the strenuous last week in the Alps, victims of days of extreme heat and cold, sickness and fatigue. Indurain survived. What also set him apart was his ability to climb despite his size. "A great carcass like that always making it so well over the mountains — incredible," Merckx, a pretty big fellow himself, said in tribute.

Indurain's major rivals were all smaller men and should have been at least his match in the Pyrénées and Alps. They had lacked his endurance, his ability to recuperate and the luck that had kept him free of sickness or accident in his 10 Tours.

"Where are they today?" asked Indurain's long-time coach and friend, José-Miguel Echavarri, referring to Bugno, Chiappucci and Rominger. "Not one of them finished the Tour. Miguel, he's still there. And still on top."

Indeed he was, glowing in his yellow jersey, as the 117 riders remaining of the 189 who set out July 2 finished on the Champs-Elysées before a crowd estimated at the usual half-million. So Indurain had much to celebrate on a hot, humid and ultimately misty day, the last in a journey covering 3978 kilometers (2474 miles).

He did smile happily after he mounted the victory podium to the familiar top step. He looked pleased — and who wouldn't? — when he received a check for 2 million French francs (about $400,000), which he always gives to his teammates. He beamed when he and the other Banesto riders took a victory lap on the Champs-Elysées, and he undoubtedly continued to beam when they were joined by friends and family at dinner and a night-club celebration later.

But really celebrate? Pop the corks on a flood of Champagne, make some noise, sass a few opponents, flirt with a wife not his own at the victory party? Not Big Mig. He didn't even whoop when the Tour crossed its last finish line.

At the end of the roundabout 175-kilometer trip from Euro Disney into the center of Paris, stage winner Seigneur finished three seconds ahead of the dejected Andreu, who bolted away from the five-man breakaway near the end of the last of eight 6-kilometer circuits of the broad avenue. Stage nine winner Hamburger was third, three seconds behind Andreu, along with the others in the breakaway: Jörg Müller, a Swiss with Mapei-CLAS, and Arturas Kasputis, a Lithuanian with Chazal. The main pack arrived 29 seconds behind Seigneur.

Indurain's total time for the Tour was 103 hours, 38 minutes, 38 seconds, an average speed of 38.383 kilometers an hour.

Ugrumov was 5:39 behind him and Pantani was third overall, 7:19 slower than the victor. Ugrumov received a million French francs ($200,000) for second place and Pantani 500,000 ($100,000), in the total prize list of 11.5 million francs ($2.25 million). Other big winners included Virenque, who won the climbers' King of the Mountain jersey and 150,000 francs ($30,000) and Abdujaparov, who won the points competition and also 150,000 francs.

In addition to his two-million-franc check, Indurain gained a stylish piece of sculpture and a secure place in the history of the sport, by matching the record of victories in four consecutive Tours. Anquetil won in 1957 and then from 1961 through 1964, and Merckx won in 1969 through 1972 and then again in 1974. When Hinault won in 1978, 1979, 1981, 1982 and 1985, he joined their club of five-time Tour champions.

Nobody is on Indurain's level with four victories. He parted company with three riders who have three victories each: Philippe Thys, a Belgian who won in 1913, 1914 and 1920, after the Tour was halted by World War I; Louison Bobet, a Frenchman who won in 1953 through 1955 … and LeMond, who won in 1986, 1989 and 1990.

It seemed fitting that Indurain should be on a level alone, since he is so unlike other champions in his lack of personality and force off the bicycle.

The Spaniard is a man of no outward flash. Unlike those riders who sport earrings or gold chains, he wears only a wedding band on his right hand, European style, and a plastic, inexpensive-looking watch.

The inner man is just as fundamental. Friends say he is humble and polite, "real" and "honest."

But after a decade of exposure as a professional bicycle racer and countless interviews since he became a star by winning his first Tour in 1991, Indurain's thoughts were known to few people.

"He prefers to listen rather than speak," says Eusebio Unzue, who discovered Indurain in a race for Spanish juniors at age 16. "No one can get inside his mind," says Pedro Delgado, Indurain's long-time friend and former teammate. There are even those who contend that he has no thoughts outside the rhythm of the sport: race, eat and sleep.

The champion's word for himself is "reserved." He used it without any sign of defensiveness in an interview with a handful of reporters before the Tour finished.

"It's true that I'm reserved and I feel a need to protect my private life," he said at one point, as he sat with little movement in his team's hotel after his dinner. "I'm a little the same on the bike as I am in life — reserved. That's the way I am and I can't change even if I wanted to. And I don't."

Do his still waters run deep? Do they run at all? He was born and reared on a farm in northeastern Spain, and a reporter for an Australian newspaper who also grew up on a farm wanted to know if that background had made him reserved. Profound and private, the questioner put it.

"It doesn't make any difference," he responded. "I know people from the country who are profound and people who aren't. The same for people from the city." He spoke Spanish, which was translated into French, the language of the sport, by a team official. Indurain's refusal to learn any other language has limited his popularity among riders, who nevertheless universally respect him.

The four reporters had decided beforehand to ask broad questions rather than ones about the Tour. Indurain the man was the quarry, not Indurain the rider.

Had reaching the age of 30 given him a new sense of panache, that dazzle he usually lacks on and off the bicycle?

"It's true that I rode a little differently at Hautacam and Luz-Ardiden," he replied, referring to the two finishes in the Pyrénées where he disposed of his main opponent, Rominger. "On the climbs, I saw that my rivals were behind, so I accelerated."

Was this Indurain the man or Indurain the rider?

Another attempt: At 30, was he a changed man?

"No, I think it's a changed race. I'm still the same Miguel Indurain, but it's another race." He seemed to be referring to the Giro d'Italia, in which he finished third after two successive victories.

Back to square one: After the Giro, was it his wounded pride that was pushing him to victory in the Tour?

"No. I analyzed what happened in the Giro and know that I wasn't yet at my best level. Here, I am. I've made a lot of progress since the Giro and I'm happy about that."

He paused, stared and elaborated: "It's not a question of motivation, but of improvement."

How did it affect him in his reserve to be an international star?

"Well, everybody knows me in Spain, that's true, but maybe not all over the world. If I go to New York, the customs officer doesn't ask me for my autograph." He had gone to New York, once, two years previously, to change planes for his honeymoon in Florida.

How important is his extended family — the parents, three sisters, brother, uncles, aunts and cousins — with whom he grew up in Navarra Province, near Pamplona?

"I have a good team, a good family, good spirit and that's all important. To be secure is important. A good entourage keeps you stable, keeps you feeling right."

For the final questions, exit Indurain the man, enter Indurain the rider.

If an American reporter could ask if he would ride in the Tour DuPont in 1995 ("We'll have to examine it, the pros and cons, and decide") the reporter for the paper in Australia could wonder if he would consider the Sun Tour there in October.

"No, not at the end of the season," he replied. "Then it's time for vacation." For the first time in nearly an hour, Indurain became animated, moving his hands in a way that seemed to mimic playing a guitar. That spontaneous gesture signaled the end of the interview.

[PART 3]

THE REMAINS OF THE YEAR

1 Glory in Sicily

A MONTH AFTER THE TOUR DE FRANCE FINISHED, IT WAS ONLY A memory, sweet to some, bitter to others … and the first major chance for revenge or confirmation was the world championships in Sicily. Miguel Indurain would not be there: He chose to train for an attack on the world hour record instead of competing in a road race that seemed designed for his strengths. Tony Rominger was also absent, recuperating, he said with a laugh, from a vacation. Greg LeMond was missing, too.

His GAN teammate Chris Boardman, however, was most emphatically present. So was another GAN rider, Francis Moreau. The two met in the final of the 4000-meter pursuit, with the Englishman coming away a runaway winner, triumphing by more than 12 seconds. Moreau, who gave so much to finish the Tour, was thrilled to take the silver medal. Boardman was equally pleased to add a rainbow jersey to the yellow ones he earned at the Tour and the one with Olympic rings he took away from the pursuit at Barcelona in 1992. Boardman said that while he might ride the pursuit event again in the world championships, his focus would be on the road.

Graeme Obree might have made the same pledge. Once again, the Scotsman was embroiled with officials of the Union Cycliste Internationale. In the spring, they banned his bicycle, effective May 1 — so he rushed down to Bordeaux at the end of April and broke Boardman's world hour record and then boasted that he had two different home-made bicycles just waiting for him to use at the world's.

At the qualifying round in the pursuit, however, the UCI struck back. After officially ratifying his bicycle, officials ruled that his saddle was illegal because it was not available on the market. When Obree replaced the saddle with a standard model, he was told an hour before his start that his position — the aerodynamic egg — was illegal. If he rode in his tuck, as he had to do with his bicycle, he would be disqualified.

Obree did ride, he did use his customary position and the UCI did disqualify him despite a top-five performance. To most, it seemed an act of spite against a rebel.

The same fortunes were played out in the first world individual time trial championship: Boardman was again an easy winner, covering the 42 kilometers in 49:34, an average speed of 50.8 kph or 48 seconds faster than an unheralded runner-up, Italian Andrea Chiurato of Mapei-CLAS. Obree was no factor. Ill, he finished a dismal 30th. Soon after, he announced that he had signed a contract with a new French road team, Le Groupement.

That team would be led by the unexpected world road race champion, Luc Leblanc, the Frenchman who had squandered his chances in the Tour. In the race at Agrigento, on Sicily's southern coast, Leblanc sped off from six companions in a breakaway and crossed the line nine seconds ahead of Claudio Chiappucci, who was so desperate for victory in front of his fellow Italians. Richard Virenque, Leblanc's fellow Frenchman and Festina teammate, took the bronze.

Leblanc's victory was hard-won and well-deserved, everybody agreed, ("He was the strongest guy there," Lance Armstrong said), but it left a slightly bitter aftertaste. Too many people remembered Leblanc's ride against his teammate Gérard Rué in the 1992 French championships and his abortive attack, destroying the chances of his teammate Laurent Jalabert, in the 1992 world championships. Out came another old story: How Laurent Fignon had been so angry that Leblanc, his subordinate, had defied team strategy to attack and take the yellow jersey for a day in the 1991 Tour. Loyalty seemed to be a minor matter to Leblanc.

Officials of the Festina team, which had rescued him and revived his career, had little to say after the world's. Leblanc had already announced that he was leaving the Andorran team for Le Groupement, citing a huge pay increase. While the Festina team would be centered now on the able Virenque, it would have been a welcome pay-back to have the world champion as its leader.

As he did so often, Leblanc voiced hurt feelings. He was unhappy, he said, to learn that Bernard Hinault, who was the last French world champion 14 years before and had coached the French road race team until the previous year, had not even bothered to watch the race on television back home.

Hinault has never been sentimental, Leblanc knew, but wasn't there a certain obligation to the sport? A few weeks later, Leblanc answered that question and enraged French race promoters by revealing that he would skip such early-season races as Paris-Nice to compete in Colombia and scout the territory where he would defend his rainbow jersey in October 1995. The fans back home would have to wait a few more weeks to see their champion.

And Armstrong? The defending world champion rode a valiant race and finished seventh, down by 48 seconds. The combined force of the French and Italian teams, which each had two riders in the final break and dominated the earlier action, was more than Armstrong could handle alone. The only other American finisher was Marty Jemison, 31st.

"I said before the race that I would not be disappointed if I don't win again," Armstrong told Rupert Guinness of *VeloNews* afterward. "I will be disappointed if I don't ride 100 percent or don't ride a smart race or if I don't give everything I have to try and win again. And when I look back at the race, I think I did everything I could. I have to be happy with seventh place. There are a lot of guys who were not there."

❀

(Although Frenchman Luc Leblanc made the biggest headlines at home with his pro road race victory, it was the story of Frenchwoman Marion Clignet that should have made a bigger impact. After all, she, too, won a rainbow jersey....)

MARION CLIGNET'S CALLING CARD IDENTIFIED HER AS A BICYCLE racer and a spokesman — two understatements. She was more than just another rider since she has been the French women's road race and pursuit champion and had just won the world women's pursuit title in Sicily. And she is more than just another spokesman, since she is a crusader.

What she crusades for is a better understanding of epilepsy. Clignet knows what some people think and say about an epileptic because she is one herself. "It's not a problem and it really shouldn't make a difference," she feels. "That's what motivates me to race: To do well because epilepsy was supposed to be an obstacle. I thought, 'You think it's an obstacle, well here we go.'"

She does indeed go. Despite a six-month ban from racing because of a disputed positive finding for caffeine, Clignet posted the fastest time in the pursuit at the 1994 world championships, winning the final by more than seven seconds. In the 1991 championships, she won the bronze medal.

Clignet raced first as an American, a distinction she earned when she was born in Hyde Park, Illinois. Since 1990, she has raced as a Frenchwoman, a distinction she earned when she was born the child of two French citizens who were living in the United States while her father taught sociology at Northwestern University.

"I have always felt very French," she said. "My family is French, I grew up speaking French in a French home. But my education is American and I have a lot of ideas that are American."

The only culture shock she reported at first was in understanding temperatures given in centigrade rather than Fahrenheit. "When they say it's 30 degrees outside, I have to transfer my thought process into the metric system," she said. Still, she quickly gives her height as one meter 70 (5 feet 7 inches) and her weight as 60 kilograms (132 pounds.). If she has any accent as she speaks English, it is the soft glottal intonation of the state of Maryland. Her parents moved there from Illinois when she was 15, when her father began teaching at the University of Maryland.

Seven years later, while she was majoring in physical education at the university, she had an epileptic seizure. That sign of neurologic disorder indirectly started her down a road that led to world championships: After her first epileptic attack, she lost her driver's license. She explained that Maryland law then decreed a year's loss of driving privileges after a seizure to determine what caused it. "Now it's down to three months," she added.

She still had to get to her job at a racquet club more than 10 miles from home, so she began traveling by bicycle. Then she started working out at the club and doing fitness programs. "One thing led to another and I got into racing," she said. It was a long step ahead for somebody who had rarely competed in organized sports other than Ultimate Frisbee.

As Clignet developed as a bicycle racer, she began campaigning for understanding of epileptics. "Basically, I wanted to educate, mostly parents of children who have epilepsy," she said. "I wanted to educate parents to be a little more liberal instead of saying, 'Oh, my God, my kid has epilepsy, he's handicapped.'

"And I wanted to inspire kids not to let it be an obstacle in the way of their doing anything they wanted to do. In the States, there was a tendency to put the kids in special-ed classes, and that would start them on a cycle where the child would think he was stupid and therefore act stupid.

"I was trying to campaign against that, but mostly educate the public."

With the support of the chemical company Ciba-Geigy, she made a speaking tour of the United States. She continued to speak in France — hence the "spokesman" on her calling card — but mainly she battled by example: The woman calling for understanding was, after all, wearing the jersey of a national or world champion.

Clignet's attitude is straightforward: Do people really discriminate against epileptics, do they really care if she is one? "I don't care if they do care," she says. "If somebody's going to treat me different because of something they can't tell I have, I don't need people like that."

She had developed a manner of introducing her illness that is based on her philosophy of, "If you present it as a problem, then it'll be a problem."

Instead, she continued, "If I have to tell somebody, I make a joke about it. I try to make them comfortable with it by letting them know I'm comfortable with it, that it's not a problem for me and it shouldn't be a problem for them. If they act weird about it, I tell them two or three of my epileptic jokes. If they don't settle down after that, I write them off."

Occasionally, there are people who have to be written off. "People have so many prejudices," she noted. One reason she shifted her base from the United States to France was her perception that U.S. racing officials downgraded her ability because of her epilepsy.

"I always wanted to move back to France for at least a year and see how it was," she said. "Would I be comfortable here? Would I make my life here? I was doing well in the States, but in terms of learning, I was at a plateau there. I couldn't progress any more racing there.

"It's not the same racing there and racing here. I race with the men here. I only race with the women internationally. Locally and regionally, only with men. I did that in the States too, but it's much harder and faster here.

"Everybody's much more experienced here. The guys I train with have been racing 10, 12 years and their fathers raced 10, 12 years. I learn stuff every day from these people. I've worked hard."

Her first victory after she moved to France, she remembered, came at the expense of the very men she trains with: "I went on a training ride with the men and I changed their attitude about women's cycling. Now they realize there are women who can race with men ... and even beat them, make them hurt in training. We've gone on lots of training rides where they've hurt more than I have. That in itself is a real victory."

2 Indurain's Hour

TRIUMPHANTLY SWITCHING FROM THE ROAD TO THE TRACK, MIGUEL Indurain broke the world hour record, the most esteemed individual mark in the sport, in Bordeaux, France, early in September. He covered 53.040 kilometers (32.96 miles), to exceed Graeme Obree's 52.713 kilometers on the same track the previous April. Obree shattered Chris Boardman's mark of 52.270 kilometers, also set in Bordeaux, in July 1993, a mark that in turn broke Obree's record of 51.596 kilometers set earlier that July in Norway.

For all Indurain's ease, the hour's ride — a man alone on the track, racing only himself and the clock — is the biggest physical and mental challenge in the sport. Since Henri Desgrange established the record of 35.325 kilometers in 1893, it had been pushed up in fractions by such champions as Oscar Egg (42.360 kilometers in 1912), Fausto Coppi (45.848 kilometers in 1942), Jacques Anquetil (46.159 kilometers in 1956) and Eddy Merckx (49.431 kilometers in 1972). Not until 1984, when Francesco Moser rode with the first modern disc wheel in Mexico City, was the 50-kilometer barrier broken.

Since then, interest in the hour's ride had waned until Obree emerged from his kitchen with his creation and startled the cycling world — and unaccountably infuriated its highest officials. Indurain's attempt was totally unlike Obree's: a major rider, a team effort, a specially crafted carbon-fiber Pinarello bicycle, international television rights — everything by the rules.

Indurain started slowly as a crowd of several thousand in the covered velodrome cheered him on. He was almost five seconds behind Obree's pace after the first five kilometers — 5:43.9 for Indurain, 5:38.99 for Obree. After 10 kilometers, Indurain was 1.9 seconds behind and after 15 kilometers just 1.1 seconds behind.

The Spaniard nearly matched Obree's time at the 20th kilometer, 22:38.54 to 22:39.03, and then began pulling ahead. At the 25th kilometer, he was 3.6 seconds faster and at 30 kilometers 5.9 seconds. By 40 kilometers, the gap was 16.9 seconds and rising.

As the hour ended, Indurain had just passed the 53-kilometer barrier. Removing his aerodynamic helmet, he punched the air with his right hand while slowing his bicycle on the wooden track.

Both Obree and Boardman were track champions, but Indurain had competed only once before on the track, in a six-hour team race in Spain a few years previously. He and his Banesto team officials devoted only three weeks to training for the attempt, which included a different bicycle and seat position than he had used in the many time trials he won in road competition.

Fears that he might have been undertrained were heightened when he got off to his relatively slow start. What he lacked in training, however, he more than compensated for in power and equipment.

❀

THE LORDS OF BICYCLE RACING — THE SELF-IMPORTANT BUNCH of businessmen and bureaucrats who are never to be confused with the athletes who actually do the riding — were wearing a big black eye. They did it to themselves, too, in the Indurain affair, the outrageous Indurain affair.

Nobody trying to despoil professional racing could have devised a better way: Choose the world championships, when people are paying attention to the sport, to accuse its main champion of taking drugs. Make it even more noticeable by leaking the news a few days before the champion would be shown on international television attempting to break one of the most respected records in the sport.

Drugs! Indurain! Wow!

"The damage is done," Indurain said. "Even if I get all the support in the world, my image has been tainted."

Yes it had … and too bad for him. The Spaniard had a pretty good image during the 10 years since he turned professional — he had never failed a drug test before the one administered in May 1994, when he won the minor Tour de l'Oise in France.

He had gone through many drug tests, of course, including the daily one in the Tour de France for the man who wears the yellow jersey. That meant a dozen tests in the last Tour de France. And a dozen the previous year, six or eight in 1992 and the same number in 1991. Throw in the daily drug tests in the Giro d'Italia for the man in the pink jersey and so add another couple of dozen in 1992 and 1993. Don't forget the random drug tests, riders chosen simply by number, in races over the years, which will add probably another half dozen. All those tests and never a suspicion.

"This is unjust, a smear campaign against Indurain, which he does not deserve," complained Eusebio Unzue, an official of the Banesto team.

Right you are, Unzue, and now it was time to bring on the next reputation to be ruined by innuendo, leak and confusion.

What facts there were appeared to be these: Indurain's urine sample showed traces of salbutamol, a chemical banned by the French Cycling Federation under the 1989 Bambuck Law, named for a former minister of sports who tried to reduce doping by athletes. The French law is stricter than the laws of the UCI and the International Olympic Committee, which usually govern the sport. International rules allow the use of salbutamol as a spray, the way Indurain used it in a medication to relieve his allergy to pollen during the spring. Under French law, an athlete may use salbutamol in a spray only on a doctor's prescription.

Officials of Indurain's team said he indeed had such a prescription. The rider himself said he had used the medication for years and had noted it in his medical dossier. A medical commission attached to the French Cycling Federation challenged these contentions and leaked the news at the world championships in Sicily.

Since he was training for his attempt in Bordeaux to break the world hour record, Indurain was not in Sicily to defend himself. Nor were his team officials. What better time to accuse him?

He is a man of few words, Indurain, but of overwhelming dignity, and he spoke of this affair with patience. "I've always tried to be honest," he said in Bordeaux, "and I will continue to abide by the rules…. Today, people are saying that I am positive. You must bear in mind that I've been taking this medicine for years. I don't know why the (French) federation is putting this out now."

Who did? In Spain, the newspaper *El Mundo* thought it did. The French wanted to prevent Indurain from equaling the record of five victories in the Tour held by Bernard Hinault and Jacques Anquetil, both Frenchman. What of Eddy Merckx, the Belgian who shared that record? *El Mundo* knew all but did not tell all.

This was just nonsense, obviously. Indurain's four Tour victories were in no way jeopardized. As he pointed out, only his reputation was damaged. The news more than a week later that a French commission cleared him of illegal activities won much smaller headlines than the news of the charge.

But what of the UCI and its many commissioners, measurers of handlebars and marketing men? Why did the UCI's officials not express loud, daily outrage at the Indurain affair? Where were they when their champion and their sport were being humiliated?

It has been said that this is a sport of suffering and sacrifice, and the Lords of Bicycle Racing seemed content to have left both to Indurain.

3 ... and Now Rominger

TONY ROMINGER WAS IN WONDERFUL FORM LATE IN THE FALL, winning first the Grand Prix des Nations, a long time trial, and then the Montjuich Hill Climb. So, almost on a whim, he decided that he, too, would attack the world hour record on the track in Bordeaux.

He would do it *his* way, however. That way was, of course, discreetly. So discreetly that when he rode on October 22, no fans were allowed in the arena and television coverage was barred. Without ceremony, Rominger cruised to a record: 53.832 kilometers — or nearly 800 meters farther than Miguel Indurain's 53.040 kilometers. "Everyone told me this would be the most excruciating effort I've ever made, but frankly it wasn't," he decided.

Less than two weeks later, he was back on the track. The numbers added up, the mathematics worked, and so it was tempting to believe that Rominger, who adores sitting at his computer to program victories on the bicycle, was certain to break his own record. Tempting, but naïve.

Rominger knew the numbers: Each push of his bicycle's enormous 60x14 gear would propel him 9.02 meters (27 feet 7 inches). If he could maintain a cadence of 102 revolutions a minute, he would travel an astonishing 55.2 kilometers (34.3 miles) in an hour. And that would outdo by nearly a kilometer and a half his record.

Check and double check. In a 27-minute test three days before his second attempt, Rominger easily exceeded his record pace and said: "Why hide it, I feel terrific. When it comes to power, I feel I've got it. I'm relaxed and confident, the record is already mine, but I'm staying concentrated and motivated."

Because the cautious Rominger rarely speaks that way, his words were respected. Nothing to it. This time, on November 5, Rominger even allowed television coverage and thousands of fans to be present. He was confident. So what if all previous challengers to the hour record spent weeks, if not months, preparing?

When he first broke Indurain's record, Rominger used what amounted to a standard steel bicycle and chose to practice on the road, not the track. For his second attempt, he had an upgraded steel bicycle ... but still a mere eight hours' experience on the boards. By the time his total reached nine, he had not just broken the record but shattered it. As Laurent Fignon, the retired winner of two Tours de France who now was a television commentator, repeatedly said, Rominger *pulverized* the record.

He covered 55.291 kilometers — 1.459 kilometers farther than his own world record and 2.251 kilometers farther than Indurain went. "Personally, I didn't think I could beat 55 kilometers," Rominger said. "I thought that if I did well, I might do 54.6 kilometers. I really hit the limits. I suffered a lot more this time than the first time."

Thrusting a microphone toward him, Fignon wanted to know if Rominger had pulverized the record because of desire. The Swiss credited concentration. "I especially tried to keep up my concentration." That and his legs as he pushed the gear that only Obree has exceeded.

Why then does Rominger surpass Indurain so easily on the track and lose to him in the time trials of the Tour de France?

Part of the answer was that Rominger is better suited to the track at 65 kilograms (143 pounds), 15 kilograms less than Indurain. And, as Fignon pointed out, the hour's ride is a solitary affair. Rominger did not have to worry that a rival — so often Indurain — would be leaving two minutes after him, learning his times at checkpoints and boring into his lead.

The pressure on Rominger could only be self-inflicted and he seemed not to have applied it in Bordeaux. As Cyrille Guimard, the head of the Castorama team and a man who has guided three riders to victories in the Tour de France, put it, "The only one who could beat Rominger? Rominger."

Stephen Roche, the Irishman who won the Tour in 1987, was another notable at trackside. "People used to say that Miguel Indurain came from another planet,"

Roche commented. "If so, where does Rominger come from?"

There was no answer. It might come in July 1996, when the Tour de France began in Brittany with Indurain again favored and Rominger again his main rival. Until then, Rominger could feast on his triumph on the track. After he completed his hour, he took some victory laps, holding up one finger — I'm No. 1 — to the few thousand fans. The boast was so atypical of Rominger that he changed to a full-handed wave before a look stole over his face and, with what for him was great audacity, he once again raised the solitary finger.

4 A New Old Jersey

LANCE ARMSTRONG WAS BACK IN HIS MOTOROLA TEAM JERSEY, a blue and red one, and only the discreet multicolored stripes at the neck and and sleeves indicated that he had ever worn the broad bands of the world champion's rainbow jersey.

"My new old jersey, yeah," he said just before the Paris-Tours classic in October. He seemed relaxed and happy, even when discussing his seventh place at the world championship road race.

"I was pleased with my race," he said. "I was outnumbered a bit: When it came down to 20-odd guys, there were seven Frenchmen and seven Italians. There's not a whole lot you can do in that scenario."

Armstrong's feelings about changing his jersey were decidedly mixed. All season, he noted that he was closely shadowed by his rivals and never allowed to attack without drawing a crowd. Now that the affable Texan was simply another rider in the pack, he felt the loss.

"I miss it," he said, speaking of the rainbow jersey. "I realize now what I had. But I'm also realistic and I realize that nobody can wear that jersey every year. If I have one year without it, I have to do my best to regain it.

"When I won the jersey it was a surprise," he added, "and I took it and wore it for a year and you don't realize at a young age, at a young point in your career, what you have. Then when you lose the jersey, you see another person wearing it, you realize exactly what it was that you achieved. And what an honor it was.

"This whole year, I knew that I was the world champion and that it was a big deal to wear the rainbow jersey. It means more now. I'm looking forward to going for it again."

Implicit in his remarks was his confidence that there would be a next time and that he would master the pressures of being world champion. Those pressures had affected his season.

"You put it down on paper and '93 was a much better year," he admitted. "Looking at it on paper. Because I had a stage victory in the Tour de France and the world championship and those are two big accomplishments. And I didn't do that this year."

His best results had been second places in the Liège-Bastogne-Liège and San Sebastian classics, second place in the Tour DuPont and the strong seventh place in the world championship.

"I'm happy with my results," he continued, "but some of the results just don't stick out. Not as much as last year. I feel I performed well in the jersey, fairly consistent. My goal was to be successful in the World Cup and I'm in a good position there now."

He ranked sixth overall in the season-long series of World Cup classics … including an undistinguished 56th place in Paris-Tours. Armstrong trained hard for the 250-kilometer race from the town of St. Arnoult-en-Yvelines, deep in the boondocks outside Paris, to Tours in the Loire Valley. Long, flat and windy, the race often ends in a mass sprint, as this one did, and that is not the young American's speciality.

"I did good training for this race and I'm extremely focused," he said beforehand. As for his form, "I think it's good."

He was looking forward to returning home to Austin and a busy off-season. "I'll be busier this winter than last year," he said. "Off-the-bike stuff."

Among other projects, he planned to help the U.S. Cycling Federation start a program to develop younger riders and expected to work as a spokesman for organizations fighting multiple sclerosis.

Also, he had an appointment at a concert with the Rolling Stones, some of whom are bicycle racing fans. "That's exactly right, November 5 in San Antonio," Armstrong said. "I'll get up on stage and jam with the boys a little bit. Then the 6th, 7th and 8th I have to be in San Francisco for a multiple-sclerosis convention."

He said that nobody close to him has the neurological disorder, but that he hoped to raise funds for research as a good citizen. "I've always been one," he said. "It's serious stuff that I do out of my own time and for absolutely nothing."

He also looked forward to the 1995 season, especially the world championships in Colombia. "I've got to be realistic and not expect to win that race every year," he repeated. "It's okay. I'm happy. But I tell you now, I'll be much hungrier before Colombia than I was before Sicily. Last year, on paper, it looks better than this year for me."

"But," he promised, "we'll be back."

✦

(Another rider looking ahead to a new season was French sprinter Laurent Jalabert, who also had his eye on the next world championships. But, in the meantime, he was making his comeback to top-line racing at Paris-Tours....)

OF COURSE HE GETS A BIT NERVOUS NOW IN THE SPRINT, LAURENT Jalabert admitted, with a defensive, lopsided grin.

Defensive because sprinters, especially first-rank ones like Jalabert, do not usually say they feel fear when a race nears its finish and dozens of riders tear for the line together in a bumping, swerving wave.

Lopsided because all his upper front teeth were missing. He lost them at the end of the first stage of the previous Tour de France, when a French policeman tried to photograph the onrushing sprint and caused a crash.

Jalabert broke his cheekbones and shattered his front teeth. Bleeding from the scalp, nose and mouth, he did not lose consciousness as the other major victim, Wilfried Nelissen, did. "Oh I remember it very well," Jalabert, 25, said before the Paris-Tours race. "I've watched the videotape; but even without it I remember what happened very well." He said he tried to hide his face after the crash so that his wife would not see on television how badly he was hurt.

Both riders were hospitalized and out of the Tour, where they were among the leading sprinters. Nelissen, at age 24 the Belgian national champion, was one of the fastest men in the sport and Jalabert, not quite so fast but perhaps savvier, won seven stages in the Vuelta a España in the spring.

After a month off to recuperate, Jalabert and Nelissen resumed racing and were among the starters in Paris-Tours. "It's long, maybe too long for me," Jal-

158

abert said before starting the six-hour race. "I still lack a little condition, but I've got the morale and maybe that will make a difference."

He regained his morale, he continued, in September at the Tour of Catalonia, when he won a stage for his first victory since the crash. Even better, he won the stage in a sprint.

"In a sprint, yes," he repeated.

The question was delicate: Did he get nervous now in the sprint, especially if he was near the front?

"A little. When a sprint starts to go really fast, when it gets dangerous, for an instant it starts to come back to me. But even if it's difficult to forget, it's over. We start sprinting and I can't let it bother me. What I think about when we start the sprint is that I have to do better than I did in the last sprint."

He shifted in his chair and tugged at his jersey. He had answered these questions before but not often.

"Something like that marks your career," he said. "But you can't let it bother you. My job is still to sprint and win races. That's what I did and I hope that's what I'll continue to do."

Unlike the Frenchman, Nelissen refused to watch the accident on videotape, and did not like to see photographs of it either. He could sound brusque when asked if he had overcome the effects of the crash.

"Yes, yes," he answered before Paris-Tours, as he fiddled with his bicycle's rear wheel. "Everything okay, no problems." He barely glanced up.

The Belgian had competed in sprints and won them, too, since the crash. Early in September, he won a criterium in Belgium and later that month he finished first in the Grand Prix d'Isbergues in France.

"That felt good," Nelissen said. "But it's a small race, not like this one here."

Paris-Tours is indeed a bigger race, a World Cup classic that often is decided by a sprint at the end of the broad and long Avenue de Grammont in Tours. So it was again in 1994.

The pack was bunched as it came down the 2400-meter-long straightaway and the sprinters were fighting and swaying for position. About 150 meters from the finish line, Frenchman Christophe Capelle of the GAN team,was bumped, put on his brakes as he headed for the steel crowd barrier and lost control of his bicycle.

Down he went … and down went five other riders behind him. They were all in the second wave of sprinters.

A few yards ahead, unaffected by the crash, the top sprinters continued to strain for the line. Riding in that group, Jalabert and Nelissen finished eighth and ninth, the highest-placed Frenchman and Belgian, as Erik Zabel, a German with Telekom, won by half a wheel.

"I lacked a little juice to finish the day well," Jalabert told a reporter for *L'Équipe*, "and I've never been so well-placed for the sprint in Paris-Tours as I was today.

"Only," he added, "there are always these little lights that flash in your head as if to say: Attention, danger."

5 An Explanation

EARLY IN DECEMBER, GREG LEMOND HAD TO SAY GOODBYE.

At age 33, he had decided that he was no longer able to compete in the sport. He would make a formal announcement a few days later in Beverly Hills, California, as part of the Korbel Night of Champions, a fund-raiser for the U.S. Cycling Federation's Olympic team.

LeMond was one of 14 male and female racers honored at a dinner afterward. Their records and medals were flashy, but none approaches LeMond's own lines in the record book: victories in the 1986, '89 and '90 Tours, victories in the 1983 and '89 world professional championship road races.

That list might have been longer but for the nearly fatal shooting in 1987 that lost him two seasons of the 14 he had been a professional. The glory years were long gone and he had not even raced since he dropped out of the '94 Tour.

"It's probably been expected," he said of his retirement. He had often reported — and displayed — weakness and exhaustion, especially in the mountains, but had been unable to specify the cause. Now he thought he could.

"It's time for me to get out because of physical problems," he explained on the phone from his home in Minnesota. "It's not just age that's been responsible for my performances these last few years. It's not that I wasn't motivated or just did it for the money.

"I have a very big physical disability that does not allow me to compete at the world-class level. I have a physical condition that is not allowing me to race at the level I should."

The condition, he continued, is called mitochondrial myopathy. "I can't spell it," he said with a laugh, "but I can say it's basically dysfunctional mitochondria, which won't help me produce energy. My energy-delivery system has been off whack. It's a mild state that affects my performance at a high level, but not my day-to-day living."

Parts of each cell, mitochondria, produce energy through respiration. When they are impaired, muscles are impaired. "I hate to say it," he continued, "but it would mimic some sort of muscular disease."

According to the Merck Manual, a standard medical reference book, mito-chondrial myopathies are among a group of progressive muscle disorders of unknown cause that are inherited through the mother. LeMond said he and his doc-tor believed, however, that the condition might have been caused by the 40 lead shot-gun pellets left in him when he was accidentally shot while hunting in California on April 20, 1987.

"It's very possible it could be the lead," he said. "We're hoping to tie it to the lead, because it would at least give me a clear answer for the future."

But he and the doctor "who has worked the last three months researching me" — Dr. Rochelle Taube of the Minneapolis Sports Medicine Center — were still not certain of the cause. "That's only the most likely theory," LeMond said.

"It seems to be caused by something when I'm racing really hard. We think it's an environmental problem, which means most likely I mobilize lead, which caus-es damage. The more I exercise, the more I mobilize it and the more damage the lead does, especially in multiday races.

"And that's why for the last three years, after four or five stages of a race I'm at a point where I need to quit racing. It's been that way for three years now."

The major effect of his ailment, he said, had been on his ability to use oxygen during a race to restore his muscles. Discussing the amount of oxygen he could use with each breath, he said, "I went from 6.2 liters of oxygen in February to 4.2 liters of oxygen during the Tour, even three weeks after the Tour.

"It makes sense now. When I was in the Tour, I kept saying 'I can't take oxy-gen in.' That's exactly what was going on. When everybody else was riding along pretty slowly and easily for them, I was riding at my max."

There it was, so terribly: The athlete betrayed by his body. Age does it, of course, to everybody, slowing us, causing pain, ruining our sleep, forcing us to step carefully down stairs that we once took two at a time. But age also prepares us by the gradual loss of strength and agility. LeMond had not been given enough time to prepare — he still believed he could control his body. Sorrowfully for him, he could not.

LeMond was not through with medical tests, which he had been having mainly in Minneapolis, near his home in Medina. "I want to get to the bottom, I want more finalized answers," he said. "This year has been the low point of my career. I have tried my hardest, mentally pushed myself beyond what I should, mentally and physically. I went through two very bad years, '92 and '93, and I was all motivated to make a charge through what would have been the last three years of my career.

"But all of a sudden the realization came to me in the Tour de France last summer that there must be something wrong — this can't be right — and that I had to revaluate whether I could continue in this sport. If I could take away the problem, I thought I could still compete."

Could he? "No," he replied, a flat and forlorn "no."

"We know it's repeated itself for the last three years. I've got a medical condition. The doctor said, 'Greg, you can feel good and you might think you've recovered, but you won't have.' No, there won't be any comeback next spring. I wouldn't be myself, the Greg LeMond of '85 or '86, where I just always felt great.

"I struggled to come back after my hunting accident. I did win the Tour in '89, miraculously I think now.

"In the last seven years, I've had four months that I felt good and in those four months I won two Tours de France and the world championship. But in the rest of those years I've been just struggling.

"I couldn't figure it out. Every year, I had different reasonings: allergies, overtraining, quarrels with my dad, this and that. There's nothing more frustrating for an athlete than to be talented and then suddenly to have that talent taken away from you.

"I never needed to race and be the last guy, getting pushed up hills. And that's who I was this year. This was a do-or-die season this year for me. I did everything I possibly could, prepared myself. Either I had to have a great season or I had to call it quits. Stop.

"The last thing I want to be considered is a rider who stayed on too long. Now I'm retired. I'll try to have fun."

His ways of having fun were long and varied, including spending more time with his wife and three children, fly fishing, downhill and cross-country skiing, tennis and golf, mountain-bike racing and searching for antiques.

"That's what I've done this fall," he reported. "I've been going to dealers for antiques, American antiques, 18th century, early 19th century. Federal period, Queen Anne period. I've been wanting to do that for years and I've never had the time."

Through his bicycle sales company, he would retain connections with the sport. He also talked about his passion for mountain-bike racing, saying he might organize a team and might even compete in a few events. Although he might also fulfill his great dream of making it to the 1996 Olympic Games in Atlanta, LeMond knew now that it would have to be as a television commentator, not as a racer in the time trial there. As of July 8, when he got off his bicycle in the middle of a Tour stage, LeMond had not been a racer.

"I want to be somewhat involved in the sport, in certain capacities, but I don't know what," he said. "I'll probably make it to the Tour next year, maybe as a television commentator, maybe as a guest. Otherwise I'll be fishing in Montana."

❋

WHEN GREG LEMOND HUNG UP, THE REPORTER HE HAD BEEN talking to went looking for a notebook in which he had written comments by Lance Armstrong earlier in the fall about LeMond's possible retirement.

Where was that notebook? Not where it should have been, atop a pile of pads and notebooks going back years, even decades, and full of brief remarks and transcriptions of tape-recorded interviews.

The notebooks were out of order. First was a brown pad and on one page, dated July 19, 1989, LeMond was saying: "It's a 24-kilometer time trial and it's not such a difficult one. It's relatively flat and downhill. I'm convinced that it's still possible. I had no idea I was going to ride this well. Really. No idea. I had some hopes I was maybe going to win a stage, maybe a top-20 finish. I was really going to be happy with that. Now I want it all. I really want to win this race."

He was sitting in his room in a hotel at L'Alpe d'Huez then, assessing his chances of overtaking Laurent Fignon, who led him by 26 seconds. This was LeMond's first Tour since his victory in 1986 and he had surprised everybody with his performance: Unveiling triathlete handlebars for the initial time trial from

Dinard to Rennes, he had won his first race since he was shot in 1987 and had donned his first yellow jersey since 1986. Another quote from the notebook, July 6, '89: "It was like winning the world championship. It was my best moment in many years. This is the most wonderful day of my life. It's almost a miracle."

Almost, but the miracle was to come on the final stage, the time trial. In second place, now trailing Fignon by 50 seconds, LeMond surged for 26 minutes 57 seconds from Versailles into Paris and the traditional finish on the Champs-Elysées. The notebook: "I didn't think; I just rode." He rode the perfect ride, the fastest any man had ever raced in the history of the Tour — 54.5 kilometers an hour (34 miles an hour). His jersey unzipped, a liter bottle of water in one hand, LeMond now watched the clock as Fignon, who left two minutes behind him, labored up the Champs-Elysées toward the Arc de Triomphe, where he would make the turn and head for the finish.

The Frenchman's 50-second lead had disappeared on the road. After 11.5 kilometers of the 24.5 in the time trial, Fignon trailed his rival's time by 21 seconds; after 14 kilometers, 24 seconds; after 18 kilometers, 35 seconds; after 20 kilometers, 45 seconds. "All I could think of was how terrible it would be to lose by one second" — LeMond.

When Fignon was 50 meters from the finish, he lost the Tour. At that point, the clock showed that he trailed LeMond by 50 seconds for the stage and that their times for the full Tour were equal — but he still had those 50 meters to pedal. The page for July 23 recorded the shout of Otto Jácome, LeMond's friend and masseur with the adr team: "You won it, Greg, you won it." Also scrawled there was Kathy LeMond's shout: "Eight seconds, Greg. You've got eight seconds less than Fignon." It was the smallest margin of victory since the Tour began in 1903.

Another notebook, from 1990: "It was my first flat of the year and it couldn't have come at a worse time. It was the first time I had no teammates with me to give me a wheel. It was the first time the team car was so far behind. It was a lot of firsts." The 17th stage of the Tour, July 18, '90. At kilometer 77, about 800 meters from the top of the Marie-Blanque Pass in the Pyrenees, the rear tire on LeMond's bicycle flatted. At that moment, Claudio Chiappucci, who wore the yellow jersey by five seconds over LeMond, attacked. By the time LeMond got a new wheel, Chiappucci was more than a minute ahead. Joined by his Z teammates, LeMond led the charge after the Italian down the Marie-Blanque. "I've never risked my life like that before, and I hope I never have to again" — LeMond. Another entry, from Jean-François Pescheux, a Tour official who followed LeMond on a motorcycle: "I've never seen a descent that fast." Slices air into zigzag with right hand. "That was the road and LeMond never braked once. He took each curve at top speed. I thought he was crazy."

After a 20-kilometer, 25-minute chase, Chiappucci was caught. Three days later, the Italian finished 2:21 behind LeMond in the ultimate time trial and surrendered the yellow jersey to the American, who wore it into Paris. His third victory in the Tour tied him with Philippe Thys, a Belgian who won in 1913, '14 and '20, and Louison Bobet, a Frenchman who won in 1953, '54 and '55.

Another notebook, this one from July 1985: "Greg knows he can ride for victory next year in the Tour. I'm just planning to have fun and make some trouble in the next Tour. All I want to do is is help one of my teammates win. If all goes well, that should be Greg LeMond." That was Bernard Hinault after his fifth Tour victory, won with a big assist from his La Vie Claire teammate LeMond, who finished second and reluctantly held up in the Pyrénées when he might have taken the yellow jersey from his leader.

The same notebook, July 20, 1985, when LeMond became the first American to win a stage in the Tour by winning the time trial near Limoges: "I'm as happy for him as if I'd won myself" — Hinault. Paul Köchli, their directeur sportif: "We've just seen a true passing of power. Greg showed he's ready to take on all the responsibilities of a team leader. Who could have hoped for a prettier end to this race?"

From a 1986 notebook: "Hinault's forgotten his promise. It looks like I'm going to finish second in the Tour again" — LeMond, July 16, the day after Hinault attacked in the Pyrénées and gained five minutes on him. The next day, after Hinault attacked again, LeMond caught and passed him on his way to victory in the final climb. A few days later, he regained the yellow jersey and was wearing it when he and Hinault steamed up to L'Alpe d'Huez together, far in front of the field. Near the top, LeMond threw an arm over Hinault's shoulder and the Frenchman raised both their hands in triumph just before LeMond slowed and allowed his leader to have the stage victory. "By finishing hand in hand, I think we gave a wonderful image of what sports are all about"— Hinault, July 21. The next morning: "I'm very proud of what we did together, but let me say it one more time: the Tour isn't over. Who was stronger in the climb? Go on, ask Greg."

"I really thought that after Alpe d'Huez, I would ride into Paris with the support of the team" — LeMond, July 24, still 2:43 up on Hinault in second place. "He made promises to me he never intended to keep. He made them just to relieve the pressures on himself. I just wish he had said at the beginning of the

Tour, 'It's each one for himself.' But he didn't and so I rode one kind of race. If he'd said, 'It's every man for himself,' I'd have ridden differently. I have bitter feelings about him."

LeMond lost only 25 seconds to Hinault in the showdown time trial and finished in Paris an easy winner of the Tour, the first American winner and the first non-European.

Other notebooks lay in the pile.

May 1986: "Superstar, that's because Hinault has been saying that about my future. Superstar — but compared to who? You can't compare me to Eddy Merckx or Bernard Hinault. I'm just Greg LeMond, I'm a different type of rider. Just because I don't have the same results as Hinault doesn't mean I'm not going to be a good rider in four or five years. I'm not Hinault. Hinault has a very strong character. He says he's going to win and he does sometimes win, but I never state that. People who don't understand think it's a complex I have, that I don't want to be first. I don't want to say premature stuff and if you don't back it up they say, 'He's all talk and no show.'"

June 15, 1984: "If I don't succeed this year, I've got five or six more tries" — LeMond, talking about his first Tour de France. "At my age, if I finish in the top three or five, I'll be happy. Not many people win it the first time out, like Hinault or Merckx." (Long pause.) "Of course I'm shooting for victory. If you don't, why race at all? You don't race the Tour de France for the experience." He finished third in his debut. In all, LeMond rode in eight Tours, winning in 1986, '89 and '90, finishing third in '84, second in '85, seventh in '91 and not finishing in '92 and '94. He missed the '87 Tour after he was shot, the '88 Tour because of tendinitis and the '93 Tour because of illness, followed by a broken wrist.

November 1987, discussing his shooting: "This accident gave me time to reorganize my life, reorganize and find out what's really important to me. Nothing's changed from what my philosophy was before, but now it's been strengthened: I'm not willing to be like Eddy Merckx and devote my life 100 percent to cycling. That isn't the only priority. You've got your work to do, and I've done it, but I'm not willing to give it 100 percent.

"This accident has allowed me to spend so much more time with my family. Otherwise, I would never have seen the birth of Scott, I would never have helped Geoffrey catch his first fish. I've gotten to be Geoffrey's Dad when before I was Daddy, the bike racer. I've spent a lot of time away from home for seven years, half your year out of a suitcase in a hotel, and now it's given me time to know and be with my family. We went on a vacation where, for the first time, I didn't give a darn what I ate, didn't worry about being in shape, didn't worry about cycling."

July 17, 1991: "I haven't given up." (Enthusiastically) "I never give up. But I'm being realistic, too. Indurain is riding unbelievably well…. The riders, except for Indurain, are just shooting for the podium and they don't give a darn about first place. That's a hard thing to accept. I don't care about second or third. It would be nice, but I'd rather have a good race and then end up second or third or fifth or sixth. Or eighth or 10th or 20th. I'd rather try to do my maximum in trying to win the race." July 23, 1991: "I can't win this race. It's over now. If there's a miracle, I might turn around overnight to become superman but there are no miracles in cycling." July 27, 1991: "I've learned that when you push yourself and win it's much easier than when you push yourself and lose." LeMond finished seventh in the 1991 Tour, the first of Indurain's four consecutive victories.

July 19, 1992: Kathy LeMond: "I'm glad it's over for his sake. He's just so exhausted. He's been wiped out." Earlier in the stage, LeMond had coasted to the side of the road, gotten off his bicycle, given up his rider's number and climbed into a team car to be driven to the finish.

November 1987: "From the start, I knew in all honesty that I was good. When I was 15 years old, I started racing in the intermediate class and as soon as I won eight or nine races, I got tired of it. I didn't want to win all the time; I liked competition. So I asked permission to race with the juniors and had a hard time at first with them, racing against 17 and 18 year olds, but I got second quite a few times. I was very competitive with that age group. I was only 15, going on 16, and I was beating guys 17 or 18 years old. When you're 25, beating guys 27 years old doesn't mean much, but when you're only a teenager, there's a huge difference with older guys in all the important areas — stamina, training, strength, experience.

"The following year, at 16, I started winning all the junior races, chalking up 30 victories a year. I'd win about half the time, lose about half the time — but losing meant getting second or third. Immediately after winning all those races, the following year, all I raced was seniors, riders 18 and over, at the national level. And then I started winning those races.

"Although I immediately had this success, I wasn't sure how good I could be. In 1977, I went to the junior world trials and won two out of three races. Although I won those two races, I couldn't be selected for the world championship team because I was too young, not yet old enough to be a junior. Then I won the national road race for juniors that year and, as I said, I started beating even national-caliber senior men. I was 16 years old when I almost beat John Howard, then the top American senior rider, in one race.

"In 1978, I kept getting better. In the spring of that year, I went to the junior world's in Washington, D.C., where I had written I wanted to get experience, and got a ninth in the road race and we got a third in the team time trial, when a team of four rides against the clock. I was the anchor guy, pretty much the strongest rider on the team. So I didn't have any doubts about my ability in America and once I got to winning at the senior level, I just wanted to move on.

"Right after that, in the summer of '78, I went to Europe for the first time. When I started racing at 14, one of the guys I raced against and became good friends with was Kent Gordis, whose Mom lived in the United States and his Dad lived in Switzerland. I arranged that summer to go with Kent for two months to Switzerland, France and Belgium and stay with his family. When we went to Europe, I started racing and winning, five or six quick races.

"That wasn't even the best of it. I still remember getting off the plane in Switzerland — it was so beautiful! I was 16 years old, but after 30 minutes there I said, 'God, Kent, I've always heard of culture shock, but there's no culture shock over here!' About a week later, I started feeling that I wanted to go home. I really started getting homesick immediately, probably 10 minutes after I said that to Kent. I realized that I had left my family and was living with a family that was used to the European way of life.

"Still there were some great moments. I remember meeting and riding with Jean-Claude Killy, the Olympic skier and a big hero of mine, and we went on a ride up to a chalet on the Joux-Plane, near the ski resort of Morzine in France. That day, on the same road, there was a stage of the Tour de France — my first sight of professional racers. On the stage to Morzine, I watched the Tour de France go by for the first time.

"I was awed. I was awed by how many people were watching the race, a couple of hundred thousand spread along the course, and by how fit the riders were. They were like gods — so thin and fit. I also couldn't believe how hard it looked."

March 20, 1992, Eddie Borysewicz, former director of the U.S. amateur team, asked if LeMond was the most talented rider he ever coached: "Yes, absolutely. Incredible talent. I saw him in '78, I said that's the diamond. That's really diamond. Only have to polish this diamond."

September 1982: "Bicycle racing isn't much of a sport yet back home. I want to help build the sport in the U.S. Maybe it'll take somebody winning the

Tour de France to do it."

Finally, the right notebook. October 1, 1994, Lance Armstrong: "I want Greg to do what he wants to do. If he wants to race again, hey, that's 100-percent fine with me. I would support him in every way. I like to be around him. If he wants to race again, then I think that's great. If he wants to retire, then I think that's great too. He can retire and say that he had a legendary career.

"He's done a lot for me whether he knows it or not or whether I know it or not. He's done a lot. He's an American and he came over here and he was the only guy really. And he didn't come over here and show his face as an American. He came over here and had a lot of success as an American. After he had success, people had to realize he was legitimate. Maybe people realized Americans can be professional cyclists, professional European cyclists. Whether he realizes it or not, he started the process. He paved the way. The road was pretty well constructed.

"I don't know how they build roads, but he cleared the trees and maybe started to lay the pavement. Maybe I'm like putting up the guard rails.

"As long as there are no red lights on this road. This is a road with only green lights."

Just one more notebook, from May 1990. LeMond had just read his biography, written after his last-stage victory in the Tour. "You really like me," (shy smile) he said — half a statement, half a question — to the writer.

Like a son, Greg, like a son.

[PART 4]

A NEW ERA DAWNS

1 Armstrong's Tour of Tragedy and Hope

A NEW SEASON BEGAN, THE MONTHS WHEELED BY AND SUDDENLY it was time for the 82nd Tour de France. Greg LeMond was not in Brittany for the start — too soon, too painful, his friends said — but Lance Armstrong certainly was. Armstrong was ready, willing and, he hoped, able. About "able," he would know in a few weeks. About "ready and willing," he had no doubts right then.

"I'm definitely fit, much more fit than I've ever been in my life, ever. I feel better, I feel stronger, my tests are better and my head is great. I'm extremely motivated, certainly more motivated for this Tour than I've ever been," he said. This would be his third Tour and the first he expected to finish.

"I think I have a better understanding of the Tour de France now, and how grand it is, and what it truly means to the sport and to the sponsors and the people. I've never been as excited about the Tour de France."

Experience was what makes the difference in his attitude, never before considered blasé. "The first year, okay, I may have been excited," he admitted. "But I had no clue, no idea what I was coming into. Last year, I may have been a bit disillusioned" — a year when he wore the rainbow jersey of the world road-race champion and was a marked man, unable to come close to a stage victory

"Now I realize what the Tour de France is about — the biggest spectacle in the sport. Cycling in July is the biggest sport in Europe. It's the ultimate in July and a great place to shine."

Armstrong intended to shine. Yes indeed.

"This year, I have some goals in mind and I'm going to be fighting," he announced. "First and foremost, I have to finish the race. I want to win a stage — the team has to win a stage." Motorola had not won a stage in the Tour since Armstrong triumphed at Verdun not quite midway through the 1993 Tour.

The Texan thought his team had an excellent chance for victory in the team time trial between Mayenne and Alençon. Third in this event in 1993 and second in 1994, Motorola, he promised, would go all out.

He returned to his personal goals: "I want to ride strongly in the time trials and the mountains. And if that all adds up to — I don't know what that adds up to in the end."

Of course he did. Less freewheeling than he was a few years ago, but just as likable, Armstrong finally came out with it.

"If I'm super, super, super, I can maybe hope to finish in the top 10. I don't know what 10th place is, normally about 20 minutes behind. If you're riding strongly in the time trials and don't have any bad luck and have just one bad day in the mountains, you can still finish in the top 10."

What about *winning* this Tour de France? It's a question usually asked by Americans who remember Greg LeMond's three victories in the Tour and expect that with LeMond retired, Armstrong would simply step up and replace him on the victory podium.

"Hah," he snorted. "You get a few questions like that, certainly. But I get a lot more about *eventually* winning the Tour de France.

"I say I'd like to contend some day and I think I can. People are quick to categorize a guy, to say he can't climb the high mountains, he can't time trial, he's too big, he can't recover." The first is often said about Armstrong and the second sometimes.

"Well, you know, you can't say that. Certainly if my development curve continues to go in the way that it's been going, there's no reason that in five years I can't contend for this race.

"I'm not in any hurry. I'm not saying I have to do it this year. Which is nice."

Armstrong returned to Europe in June from the United States, where he won the Tour DuPont and the West Virginia Kmart Classic, to ride in the Tour of Switzerland, where he was fourth in the prologue and fifth in the uphill individual time trial. Both were among his best results in similar European races.

"I feel a lot stronger than I did a year ago," he said. The reason, he explained, is "I'm another year older.

"I expect that progress. Just as I expect a year from now I'll be stronger than I am this year. I'm only 23 years old. I fully expect to have steps like that for the next five years. That's reasonable, that's natural and normal.

"Mentally, I'm much better than I was three or four months ago. More focused." Credit for that went to his "very satisfying" victory in the DuPont, in which he finished second the previous two years. Armstrong likes to win and he likes to win in the United States.

In the Tour, he said, the daily stages that offered him his best chances to win came during the second week, on the three stages between the Alps and the Pyrénées.

He flipped through some cards showing the profiles of each day's course. "I really like this day," he said, referring to the 12th stage, from St. Etienne to Mende. "Look at that finish," a short, sharp climb.

"I like this one too," the 13th stage, from Mende to Revel. "It'll be hot and I like that and all these ups and downs, I like that."

He turned over a few more cards, their jagged profiles showing the mountains to be labored up, the descents to be sped down.

"It looks pretty easy this year, the Tour de France," Armstrong decided.

He paused a beat and smiled. "I don't think so," he said.

❁

AND, OF COURSE, IT WASN'T EASY. ESPECIALLY NOT AFTER A Motorola rider, Fabio Casartelli, a 24-year-old Italian bicycle racer who was the reigning Olympic road race champion, was killed when he crashed on a steep and sinuous descent in the Pyrénées and fractured his skull.

While being flown by helicopter to a hospital in Tarbes, Casartelli's heart stopped three times. He was revived by doctors aboard the craft after the first two attacks, but they were unsuccessful after the third and he could not be helped at the hospital either.

The death was the third in the history of the Tour de France, which began in 1903, and the first since 1967. Tom Simpson, a British rider contending for overall victory, died that July of heat asphyxiation, complicated by amphetamines, while climbing Mont Ventoux in 100-degree heat. In 1935, Francisco Cepeda of Spain died after a fall, while descending the Col du Galibier in the Alps.

Casartelli crashed on the descent from the Col de Portet d'Aspet, the first of six climbs on that stage in the Pyrénées. As riders approached speeds of 70 kilometers an hour, seven of them, including Casartelli, failed to negotiate a left-hand curve. He flew into the air and smashed the right side of his head, apparently against one of the low, concrete blocks lining the road high above a valley.

"It was a fairly fast descent," said the French rider François Simon, who was behind Casartelli. "At a certain point, there was a longer curve than the others. Casartelli couldn't make the turn. I think it was his back wheel which hit the side, and he flew in the air."

Tour doctors quickly examined the Italian and determined that he had major injuries. Dr. Gérard Nicollet, one of the Tour's four doctors, and Dr. Massimo Testa, the Motorola team's doctor, accompanied the rider and tried to save him on the helicopter.

"I arrived 10 seconds after the fall," said Gérard Porte, the Tour's chief doctor. "I could tell it was a serious injury. Casartelli had cuts that were bleeding badly. We did everything in the best conditions and as fast as we could. But he had very serious cuts, and when there's such heavy bleeding you know it was a very powerful impact."

Three other riders were badly injured in the crash. Dante Rezze, a Frenchman with the AKI-Gipiemme team, went off the road and into the trees, fracturing his left leg. Dirk Baldinger, a German with Polti, also fractured his left leg but, like Casartelli, did not hurtle off the road. Less seriously injured was Juan Cesar Aguirre, a Colombian with Kelme, although his injured shoulder forced him to withdraw from the race later in the stage.

Casartelli was not wearing a helmet, whose use is not mandatory in European pro racing, except in Belgium and the Netherlands. Even there, the riders can use "hairnet" helmets — strips of leather, rather than more resistant hardshell gear.

Despite the obvious dangers, few professional riders wear helmets on hot days — as this one was. They say that for comfort's sake they prefer cloth caps or bare heads. When international officials tried to make helmets mandatory in 1991, the riders protested at a number of spring races, and threatened to strike. The officials backed off.

The accident occurred at kilometer 33 of the 206-kilometer-long stage from St. Girons to Cauterets. Race drivers were warned beforehand that the descent was especially dangerous because of its many short curves and steep grades. Casartelli crashed at 11:48 a.m. and his death was announced on the Tour's internal radio at 2:39 p.m. by Jean-Marie Leblanc, the director of the race.

In his first year with Motorola, Casartelli rode previously for the Ariostea and ZG teams in Italy. After winning the gold medal in the Olympic race, he turned professional in 1993 and won a stage of the Settimana Bergamasca and twice finished second in stages of the Tour of Switzerland. He was well liked throughout the peloton, and his upbeat personality was greatly appreciated by his new colleagues.

⊛

THE NEXT DAY, STUNNED, SADDENED AND IN SOME CASES demoralized by his death, the 119 remaining riders turned the stage into a tribute to Casartelli by common consent, from Miguel Indurain in the yellow jersey to Hector Castano, the *lanterne rouge*.

Armstrong and his Motorola teammates did not abandon, as some thought they might. "The team decided to stay in the race for the memory of Casartelli," said Paul Sherwen, Motorola's public relations director and a former Tour rider. "They felt it was easier to stay together as a group than to split up and go home each his separate way. Even if they didn't race today, they'd still have to race next week or the week after."

But this 16th of the 20 stages was not a race. It was a procession. The pack's leaders decided early in the day that all riders show solidarity for the memory of Casartelli, and so they remained grouped throughout, traveling at 30 kph, about 2 kph below the expected average speed for this mountainous course.

In the same spirit, Casartelli's six remaining Motorola teammates were allowed to ride out ahead at the finish, and Andrea Peron — a fellow Italian and Casartelli's roommate — was permitted to cross the finish line first.

The team wore black patches pinned to their left sleeves. Applauded by a huge crowd of spectators before the start, the six riders took their places in the front line as the pack observed a minute of silence for their dead teammate.

Shoulder to shoulder, rank after rank, the riders then traveled the 237 kilometers from Tarbes to Pau over six climbs in the Pyrénées. Attacks were forbidden, and riders who fell behind on the climbs were given time to catch up — although two dropped riders were too tired to chase back, and had to quit.

With about 10 kilometers to go, the rest of the pack let the Motorola riders move to the front. When one of them, Stephen Swart, had to stop because of a flat and have a wheel replaced, the entire pack slowed to await his return. In the final few kilometers, the six rode alone as the rest of the pack dropped a few hundred yards back. Abreast as the finish line approached, the Motorola riders coasted over together with Peron first, in an immensely moving culmination of an emotional day. All other placings, from second to 117th, were irrelevant. The pack was one man in this stage.

The same sort of gesture was made in 1967, the day after Simpson died. The next day, the pack allowed his teammate and countryman, Barry Hoban, to go on ahead to win in a solo breakaway.

In addition to the tribute of victory for Peron, the peloton decided that all the prizes for the day would be donated to Casartelli's widow Anna Lisa and infant son Marco. That sum was matched by the Tour's organizers, for a total donation of about $95,000. Furthermore, the Motorola team said it would turn over all its prize money from the Tour, about $57,500, to the widow.

❋

IN AN EMOTIONAL RIDE TWO DAYS LATER, ARMSTRONG PAID HIS personal tribute to Casartelli: He won the stage into Limoges, blowing a kiss to the heavens, and saying that his ride had been inspired by and dedicated to his teammate.

"This was for Fabio Casartelli," the Texan said. "I was very, very bad in the last bit, but I kept thinking of him. I did it for one person."

Armstrong attacked his 12-man breakaway at the top of the last climb, built a lead that topped a minute, and arrived at the finish line 33 seconds ahead of the runner-up. With a kilometer to go, he looked back and saw no opponents. He pointed to the sky with his right hand, then both hands and finally blew a kiss upward.

"Everybody loved him," he said of Casartelli. "He was a super person, he had more friends than anybody I've ever known."

One of the Texan's collaborators in the breakaway, Laurent Dufaux, a Swiss with Festina, paid his own tribute to Armstrong: "He attacked at the right moment and he was just too strong today." The victory avenged Armstrong's second place in a two-man sprint into Revel a week earlier.

At kilometer 83, six riders jumped away from the pack after a frenzy of earlier attacks. They were joined shortly by six more, including Armstrong. Since 10 of the race's 21 teams were represented in the move, the chase after them was minimal. The 12 were not allowed, however, to build a huge lead. Just after the King of the Mountains sprint on the final climb, Armstrong caught his companions unawares with a lightning-fast attack.

He bolted off and rode the final 29 kilometers alone. "I didn't like my chances in the sprint and I thought I'd better try to put them away early," Armstrong said. "I had a feeling that they couldn't put a chase together." They couldn't.

❋

ANOTHER TWO DAYS LATER, THE TOUR WAS RIDING INTO PARIS, finished, with Miguel Indurain the easy victor for an unprecedented fifth consecutive year. Much earlier, he had also won over at least one doubter. Armstrong, who pronounces himself Indurain's biggest fan, had a small suspicion before the Tour began that the Spaniard could not set that record.

"The numbers, I'm aware of the numbers," Armstrong said. "If I'm playing the numbers, it's never been done."

Now it has. Indurain joined Jacques Anquetil, Eddy Merckx and Bernard Hinault as the only riders ever to win the Tour five times. Since the race began in 1903, he is the only man to win it five years running.

That convinced Armstrong that numbers are overrated.

"He's won five in a row and I say he'll win seven in a row," the American said as he turned in his bicycle to mechanics outside his hotel after the finish. A similar prediction that the 31-year-old Indurain may be unbeatable for two more Tours was made the next morning by Hinault and Merckx in the pages of *L'Équipe*, the French daily sports newspaper.

"He's great; he's super," Armstrong said with enthusiasm about his role model. "He's the biggest engine ever to hit the sport. He's one of the classiest guys out there. He's too good, too good.

"He's too professional. His team is too professional. He's got it down. I could be wrong, but I'm now saying seven in a row."

Armstrong was in an expansive mood after the finish, having fulfilled two of his three goals: He finished and he won a daily stage although, in 36th place overall, he failed to reach the top 15. That was the lowest-rated goal anyway, and so Armstrong was happy to be signing autographs, posing for pictures with fans and accepting congratulations for his stage victory, for finishing the Tour for the first time in three rides, and for dealing so admirably with the death of Casartelli.

Life is a learning experience, agreed, and Armstrong said he had learned a lot during the previous three weeks about professional bicycle racing and about life itself.

"In cycling, I learned what it's like to do a three-week race," he explained. "Hard, very hard. But the last few days I felt so good that I think I'm coming out of this race in a good way.

"The race did a lot for me in terms of riding three weeks. People say once you do a big Tour, then you're a different rider. It changes you. I do expect it to give me some strength. I'm certainly coming out of the race healthy."

An American couple pushed up to him and the woman told him: "We're very proud of you. You represent us well."

"People are nice," the Texan said.

That brought him to Casartelli's death.

"Certainly I learned more about life and death in this Tour than I learned about bike racing," he said. "I never had to deal with the death of a family member, a friend, a teammate ever before. Ever. This is the first one. And to have it happen in the Tour de France, it was very difficult."

He handled it well, a friend said, citing the way Armstrong pointed to the sky at the end of the stage victory.

"I didn't ..." Armstrong began. "I didn't ..."

Then he found the words: "That was a special day. Those weren't my legs. Because they were way too good. They were so good.

"The week before that, I was physically so tired and the legs that day, they showed up, the breakaway showed up and that attack I made — in the last 25 kilometers, to go 55 to 60 kilometers an hour on a false-flat uphill....

"Come on," Armstrong continued, "I've never in my life ridden a bike that fast. Those were very special kilometers there.

"It's hard to explain; it's unexplainable. The feeling was ..."

A long pause. "Boy," Armstrong said, "I was so strong."

Epilogue: Unforgettable!

MONSIEUR PATRICK, OWNER AND MANAGER OF A HOTEL ON THE
Place du 11 Novembre in Saugues, France, was tending bar one July evening and cheer-fully explaining the difficulties of his chosen career.

"Down here at 7 in the morning to serve the guests' breakfasts, closing at 1 in the morning," he said as he wiped glasses, steamed milk for coffee, poured wine and drew a few beers. "Sometimes a guest wants to leave at 6. Where do you buy croissants at that hour? You have to buy them the night before and store them in the refrigerator.

"Vacations? We've taken eight days off in the two years since we bought the hotel. When can we go? In the spring and summer, it's the tourist season. In the fall, it's the ban-quet season."

By "banquet," he possibly exaggerated. The restaurant attached to his hotel adver-tises on its awning crêpes and pizzas. The town of Saugues is in the Auvergne, a region in central France not well-known for its cuisine, but even such local delicacies as stuffed cabbage, duck breast with blueberries or almost anything with chestnuts qualify better as banquet fare than a pizza.

"In the banquet season," he persisted, "we serve up to 250 people a day. Other-wise 150.

"Days off? You can't close a hotel one day a week. Bills to be paid: The hotel had 25 rooms when we came here, we knocked down walls, made it into 18 rooms, fixed the plumbing, put in an elevator." He rubbed his thumb over his first two fingers in the familiar gesture.

"No vacations, no days off, down here at 7, up to bed at 1," he said in good-natured

summary. "*And the worst? The worst is that I don't even get to watch the Tour de France on television.*

"*Too busy. Too busy even for the Tour de France.*"

For the first time in his monologue, his face lost its smile. The rare bartender telling his troubles to a customer, he seemed distraught. If there had been a drink in front of him, somebody would have offered to fill it up again.

"*The Tour de France could come right past the hotel,*" *he continued,* "*and I couldn't even watch it on television.*"

The Tour *indeed remains a benchmark in the heartland,* la France profonde. *The bicycle race is in distant Brittany or the Alps, and people in other regions watch on television. More than 40 million French viewers see the race on television, the organizers of the Tour say. If the bicycle race rolls through or near town, people turn out. Fifteen million people flock to the sides of the Tour's roads, according to the organizers.*

What else is there to do in a pleasant town like Saugues? Four concerts were scheduled that summer, not including the accordion festival on August 13. There would be two conferences to discuss a local legend, the Bête du Gévaudan, a sort of werewolf, it seems, to whom or which a museum is being built. The lamb fair lay ahead and, two days later, the mushroom festival — featuring "the biggest mushroom in the world." The rest, as a Dane said, is silence.

The next morning, some of the people of Saugues were up early. Four old men in the sort of caps that old men wear were gathered in the Place du 11 Novembre outside the hotel, talking about the Tour de France. A Frenchman, Laurent Jalabert, had won the previous day's stage in a grand exploit *on Bastille Day, the national holiday, and the four old men were feeling particularly proud to be French that morning.*

"*The Tour de France came here a few years ago,*" *one of them told a visitor.* "*This town, Saugues. The Tour.*"

The daily stage ended or started here?

"*No, it came here. Passed through. This town, Saugues. The Tour.*"

Who won that stage? He didn't know. Who won that Tour? He couldn't recall. All he could remember was that the Tour had come through town. This town.

"*Unforgettable,*" *he said.*